PAD gave to Evelyn V. to send to me 9/2011

What Leaders Are Saying about
TEN and Terry Smith

TEN by Terry Smith is a must-read for coaches, players, leaders, or anyone who doesn't want to settle for an average or just OK future. It inspires and reveals deep truths and strategies that will help us understand and move toward our potential in Christ to create a better future for ourselves and others.

> Willie Alfonso
> Chaplain, New York Yankees and New Jersey Nets

There is no way in the world you can read this book without being challenged. You will want more, be more, and do more.

Terry has struck a note—a chord—for leaders and potential leaders. *TEN* is a part of the natural order that often people miss because they limit themselves. This book will put you in the right orbit so that you will reach your full potential.

> Archbishop LeRoy Bailey, Jr.
> The First Cathedral, Bloomfield, CT

Just when it seems everything has been said on leadership, Terry Smith starts a new conversation. *TEN* dares each of us to reach for God's design—to actualize our potential to influence our own and others' futures. This uniquely hopeful voice will change your perspective on your need for significance. We devoured it! Definitely one of the best books we've read in years. A "must-read."

> Steve Bell
> Executive Vice President, Willow Creek Association
>
> Valerie Bell
> Author and speaker
> Chairman of the Board, MOPS International

If you are looking for significance in your life, you must read *TEN*. Terry Smith will show you how God works with you and through you to open up possibilities you never knew existed. This book is full of hope.

>   Ken Blanchard
>   Co-author of *The One Minute Manager* and *Lead Like Jesus*

If you are as passionate as I am about creating a better world, then this book will instruct and inspire you. Terry's ideas have motivated and helped me. You are going to love *TEN*.

>   Cory Booker
>   Mayor, Newark, NJ

TEN is an insightful book on how to create a fuller future for yourself and your family. Terry Smith shows us how to want more than the ordinary—to not settle for what we have. I first heard of the reverend from my father, who said this young man was going to do a lot of great things...and he was right.

>   Richard J. Codey
>   Former New Jersey Governor
>   Senator, State of New Jersey

TEN is a must-read! In this book, my pastor, Terry Smith, perfectly balances humility and patience toward God's will for our lives while quietly whispering in our ears the idea that God has more in store for each of us. Here's to being open to the possibilities!

>   Jerricho Cotchery
>   New York Jets wide receiver

Most speakers have a "life message" that they were born to share. I think this is Terry's. He inspires me on this theme of destiny and purpose like few people I know. Get ready to amp up your passion for living!

>   Shawn Craig of Phillips, Craig, and Dean
>   Senior Pastor, South County Christian Center

In today's world, with so many people feeling stuck in their lives, Pastor Terry Smith's book *TEN* comes as a breath of fresh air. He clearly shows us how we can live the life that God has always intended for us. The world needs this book.

> Xavier Davis
> Pianist
> Instructor at the Juilliard School

Terry Smith has been my friend for twenty-five years. Early on, I came to realize that his skills as a communicator were something uniquely special. His creative thinking and innovative perspective have challenged me to become a better leader, a better husband, a better father, and a better Christian. It is now my hope that by reading this book you will discover Terry's unique gifts as well.

> Dan Dean of Phillips, Craig, and Dean
> Senior Pastor, The Heartland Church, Carrollton, TX

Terry Smith will inspire you to take "life by the horns" and create the future God intended for you. Terry's expertise and leadership tools have provided a wonderful framework for me over the years. This book is a great resource to enlighten, improve, and challenge yourself while leading others into the same reality! *TEN* is an absolute must-read for anyone in leadership.

> Pastor Michael Durso
> Senior Pastor, Christ Tabernacle

Pastor Terry Smith shows us that getting to know God is also about getting to know ourselves. He inspires us to think and act more boldly in our personal, professional, and spiritual journeys so that we become the leaders God longs for us to be. I read this book on the plane. Despite some great in-flight movies, I couldn't put it down!

> Priyan Fernando
> President and Chief Operating Officer, American Express
> Business Travel

Terry Smith does not only inspire people to a preferred future—the real and true future in God's mind—but he seems to address the question most people ask in their hearts and minds and get anxious about: "What does the future hold for me?"

Terry walks his talk. *TEN* comes with refreshing sparks similar to *A Purpose Driven Life* by Rick Warren. Terry's anecdotes, illustrations, and living examples make this book such fascinating, exciting, and inspiring reading. The young in particular must read this and not miss out!

> Nathan Gasatura
> Bishop of the Diocese of Butare, the Anglican Church of
> Rwanda
> President Emeritus, Rwanda National HIV/AIDS Control
> Commission

Surveys reveal that Americans are in a somber mood and are apprehensive about the future. *TEN* is a timely and much-needed book that gives readers fresh hope, reminding them that God has a special future for each of us. Author Terry Smith's rise in ministry is living proof of what can happen when we seek the future God has in store for us.

> George Gallup, Jr.
> Founding chairman, George H. Gallup International
> Institute, Princeton Religion Research Center

If you want more out of life but have not found the right key, you must read Pastor Terry Smith's book *TEN*. This book is a must-read for counselors, teachers, pastors, and individuals searching for the right combination of things to get people where they want to go. Smith shows how God is the answer to getting one to the next level.

> W. Wilson Goode, Sr., D.Min.
> Director of Amachi
> Former Mayor of Philadelphia, PA

TEN is the guidebook for the journey—the wisdom for the future—for those who serve and those who seek to serve. To serve is to live.

> Frances Hesselbein
> Chief Executive Officer, Girl Scouts of the USA
>   (1976–1990)
> Recipient of the Presidential Medal of Freedom
> President and Chief Executive Officer, Leader to Leader Institute

How many times have we heard someone say, "Live life to the fullest"? What does this mean? I believe if most people would consider this possible, we would want to find out. Pastor Terry Smith challenges us to consider asking God to help us realize that He intended this for us. Choose abundant life. Choose *TEN!*

> Allan Houston
> Former NBA All-Star
> Assistant General Manager, New York Knicks

This challenging book will raise the bar for leaders in every walk of life.

> Bill Hybels
> Senior Pastor, Willow Creek Community Church
> Chairman of the Board, Willow Creek Association

My father was a Nazarene pastor. He taught us at a very young age not to believe in men but in God. But when I heard Pastor Terry Smith preach for the first time, I felt that God was communicating through man. My faith became stronger.

> Wyclef Jean
> Grammy Award–winning artist and humanitarian

No matter what successes you enjoy or what is going on in your life, Terry Smith provides the tools to get more out of your life and lessons for enriching the quality of life to create an enduring future. He has been an enormous source of strength and insight for me, both personally and professionally.

> Robert D. Parisi
> Mayor, Township of West Orange, NJ

Having journeyed with Pastor Terry Smith for the past fifteen years, I have witnessed how he embodies the message of his book as an extraordinary communicator. His life and leadership have breathed possibilities into the lives of thousands of people in the Metro NYC region. I strongly encourage you to read this book and lead others through its message.

Dr. Mac Pier
President, New York City Leadership Center

Through an interesting mixture of examples from the secular and non-secular world, Terry Smith inspires readers to reach beyond their perceived limitations, enhancing their lives as well as those around them. Finish *TEN* and soar!

John F. McKeon
Deputy Majority Leader, New Jersey State Assembly
Former Mayor, West Orange, NJ

TEN encourages you to open your heart to new possibilities and your mind to dreams deferred. It will motivate you in a God-inspired way to grow more, do more, give more, and achieve more than you ever imagined.

Connia Nelson
Senior Vice President, Verizon Telecom and Business

Pastor Smith's book *TEN* is a fascinating book that makes you see the world in a different way—God's way. This book is very encouraging, and I recommend it no matter where you are in your journey.

Roman Oben
NFL Super Bowl champion, television personality, and
radio commentator for the New York Giants

Precious lessons and sound principles to a better you, a preferred future you, and a miracle you. In this book, Pastor Terry shares how God can and will work wonders in your life if you allow Him to. There is no limit to His wisdom, power, and grace! Read this book and be changed!

Jenny Sim
Vice President of Finance and Strategic Planning, Footlocker

TEN

HOW WOULD YOU RATE YOUR LIFE?

TEN

HOW WOULD

YOU RATE YOUR LIFE?

TERRY A. SMITH

HIGHERLIFE
DEVELOPMENT SERVICES, INC

Oviedo, Florida

TEN: How Would You Rate Your Life?
by Terry A. Smith

Published by HigherLife Development Services, Inc.
400 Fontana Circle
Building 1—Suite 105
Oviedo, Florida 32765
(407) 563-4806
www.ahigherlife.com

Dedication

To my parents, Delton and Jean Smith,
who inspired me to say yes to possibility.

To my wife, Sharon,
who inspires me.

To my kids—Sumerr, Caleb, and Christian—
who I hope I have inspired,
and who I hope to continue to inspire
to create the best possible future for themselves and others.

TABLE OF CONTENTS

Preface

I'VE COME TO THINK that Someone is cheering for us as we move toward our best future. That an Audience is watching and applauding and shouting our names.

In 2005, my wife Sharon ran the New York City Marathon, her first marathon. It was a pretty big deal in our family. Sharon has spent a lot of time in her life cheering for each of us, literally and figuratively. This was our chance to cheer for her. If you know anything about preparing for a marathon, you know that she had to train incredibly hard for many months.

The marathon took place on a Sunday, and we had decided that I could be at our first morning service at the church where I serve in a suburb of New York City and leave directly from there to cheer for Sharon at the eighth mile marker.

Accompanied by our kids and some friends who were familiar with maneuvering through the city's subways and streets, we jumped on a train that took us into the city. After much time and effort elbow-battling the adrenaline-pumped and boisterous crowds, we finally stood at the prearranged marker waiting for Sharon. After twenty minutes of watching thousands of athletes pass by, we came to the horrible conclusion that we had missed her. Sharon was running faster than we had anticipated, which was, in itself, a good thing. But it was disappointing to us that we couldn't see and support her. More importantly, I knew that she had planned on seeing us there and had to be crushed when she didn't.

We quickly figured out that the next opportunity to see her was at the seventeenth mile marker. Three subway connections later and after running our own mini-marathon, we ended up at what was probably the most crowded place in New York City. Around us were tens of thousands of people crunched together like sardines, screaming words of encouragement to their loved ones. As a pretty aggressive guy, I managed to wrestle my way to the front, right to the divider, probably hurting some innocent bystanders in the process. Not five minutes later I saw her. She had stopped to get a drink of water, but she was on the opposite side of this expansive street! Not about to be discouraged, I yelled her name at the top of my lungs and waved my arms like a maniac trying to get her attention. At one point she lifted her head and looked around, but—not aware of us—she quickly put her head down and kept on running.

At that moment, I was flooded by an inexplicable desperation. I knew Sharon needed to see us, and we needed to see her. So I did what any normal, reasonable, and supportive husband would do. I took off running again down the sidewalk to try to catch up with her. I probably shouldn't say this, but I really didn't care who or what was in my way. They were all going down! I climbed up on a barricade at one point and shouted, "Sharon, Sharon, Sharon!" but she had already passed. It was terrible! As I got down from the barricade, I realized I was totally separated from my kids and the other folks who were with us. I didn't have my cell phone and was basically lost. But it didn't matter; I knew our group would find each other eventually. I had to find Sharon. I flagged down a police officer who, sensing my despair, suggested that the next reasonable place to see her would be in Central Park, close to the finish line.

So I took off again, this time in a full-fledged sprint, toward the park across Manhattan. I had never run so hard in my life! By the time I got there, I was literally soaking wet, my stomach was growling from hunger, and I had to use the restroom. But I found a place at the twenty-fifth mile marker and stood there for an hour and twenty minutes, waiting for my wife. After watching thousands more people plod by, I finally saw her. Her head was down, she was obviously exhausted and in tremendous pain, and as she trudged toward my position, I screamed out her name. "Sharon! Sharon!" In an indescribably beautiful moment, her eyes met mine. I jumped out from the sidewalk, told her how badly we had wanted to see her, and started to encourage her. I ran the last mile with her, jumping out before the finish line.

Here is part of what I learned that day. Though I already understood how much Sharon needed her family to cheer for her, what really surprised me was how much I needed to cheer for her. I needed her to hear me yell her name, to know that I was for her, to know that I loved her.

I'm reminded of the line in the romantic comedy *Shall We Dance?* in which a wife suffering a discouraging time in her marriage was asked by a cynical advisor why she believed in the ideal of marriage. She answered, "We need a witness to our lives... in a marriage, you're promising to care about everything. The good things, the bad things, the terrible things, the mundane things... You're saying, 'Your life will not go unwitnessed, because I will be your witness.'"

I learned that day how badly I needed to be a witness, a supportive, yelling-like-a-lunatic, I-know-you're-tired-and-feel-like-giving-up-but-you-can-do-it kind of a witness. Now here's my point. It might sound a little crazy, but I believe God is desperate to cheer us to our futures. He is the ultimate witness to our lives. He is our primary audience, and He wants us to hear Him shouting our name.

It's like that final scene in *The Gladiator* where a battered, bloodied, and bruised Maximus stands in the Colosseum, barely able to keep from collapsing. He has defeated the most vicious gladiators in the empire, and he's won the favor of the tens of thousands in the crowd. They start to chant his name with a deafening roar. "Maximus! Maximus! Maximus!"

reverberates throughout the stadium. See, I think God is that kind of an audience.

Can you hear His voice—"like the roar of mighty ocean waves or the rolling of loud thunder"—shouting your name (Rev. 14:2, NLT)? Listen. Listen carefully. Listen with your heart. Hear Him calling to you. He sees it all. He has witnessed your victories. He is aware of your defeats. He wants your God-inspired dreams to come true. He wants you to help make His world all He knows it can be. He is for you. Cheering for you. And if God is for us, then how can we do anything but believe that our best possible future is within our grasp? It is. Better life than we can even imagine is just ahead. And God wants it for us even more than we do.

Introduction

What Do You Want?

I DON'T THINK PEOPLE want enough.

An opinion piece in the *New York Times* claimed that most of our problems result from wanting too much. I couldn't agree less. I think we should want more.

Not more stuff. More life. And not just for ourselves but also for others.

Jesus Christ said that His purpose is to give us "life—life in all its fullness" or "more and better life than [you] ever dreamed of" (John 10:10, NCV, MSG).

Why would He say that if we aren't supposed to want it?

The "more and better life than you ever dreamed of" is the future that exists in God's mind. It's the dream He has for us. We can tap into this dream and create a preferred future for ourselves and others.

If we want to.

A seminal moment in my life happened when I was eighteen years old. I spent some time with a middle-aged man who was living a relatively uneventful life. He'd experienced moderate success in a career centered on helping people. He had a nice wife and nice kids and a nice house. He was a good and decent man. I liked him a lot.

One day, in kind of a dramatic way, he tried to offer me some life advice from his personal story. "Terry," he said, "I never asked God for too much. I just told Him I wanted a nice, quiet life and to be able to help a few people along the way. And I told God that I didn't want to suffer too much. That's exactly what I have." I was only eighteen, but at that moment I knew that I wanted more. Maybe instead of telling God what was in his mind, this nice man should have asked God what was in His. I bet God was thinking *more*—more than this guy had ever dreamed of.

I don't think many people launch their lives wanting to be average. Regardless, that's where many of us land. I don't think wanting less is our God-given first instinct. Somehow, we learn to want less along the way.

You may feel that you are living a life that is good enough. You may be well-educated, employed by a Fortune 500 company, and involved in a life-changing volunteer organization in your community. But there's even more out there. Open to the possibility that there are dreams and purpose and meaning inside of you—opportunities you're not yet aware of.

Or you might be someone who feels your life is not successful and are altogether unfulfilled. You are unsatisfied with how things are turning out and may not be sure if more exists. Many people are bound by a survivor's mentality because they cannot understand the opportunity to partner with God in creating inspired futures and, ultimately, a better life for themselves, those they love, and even for the world. These bigger and better concepts never materialize because they believe God moves only in capricious whims, snapping His fingers to make things happen. Some would say that a human being's destiny is to be a puppet to God, the grand puppeteer.

That view is sad. And incorrect. Our true Creator births visions and ideas in our minds and gives us the will to do something about it!

When I write about God-inspired futures, I frequently use the words "better," "best," and "preferred." *Better* is more than you have at the present. It doesn't mean that what you have is necessarily bad, just that it's less than what is possible.

Best is even better than better. On a fulfillment scale of one to ten, you may have a present experience of, let's say, a seven. An eight would be better, but it's not best.

Best is a *TEN*.

In my worldview, a *TEN* is defined by the gospel of John, chapter *TEN*, verse *TEN*. I've already referred to it. It's the verse that talks about life in all its fullness. The more and better life. Abundant life. Until we can describe the whole of our lives like this, we are experiencing less than what's possible. I believe you can experience the best possible future.

And this future is a preferred future. It's the future you choose to create, not something forced on you. The future *you* prefer. The future *you* want. Your will is involved.

Then there is an even deeper level of understanding that is necessary to "better," "best," and "preferred": a God-inspired future is also a "good" future. I mean this in a moral sense. A good future is about doing life as God intended it to be done. It's knowing that when we do, life is more desirable in every way. A preferred future is not primarily about how we feel or what we have. It's about wanting what's right.

Thank God for people who have had a highly stimulated "want to." History doesn't have much to say about nice people who live nice lives. History talks about people who wanted more.

John Adams, one of the fathers of the United States and its second president, was an incredibly ambitious young man. He was also a deeply moral man who desperately wanted to do something great with his life:

> He felt "anxious, eager after something," but what it was he did not know.... "I have...a strong desire for distinction."
>
> "I never shall shine, 'til some animating occasion calls forth all my powers." It was 1760, the year twenty-two-year-old George III was crowned king and Adams turned twenty-five....

"Why have I not genius to start some new thought?" he asked at
another point in his diary. "Some thing that will surprise the world?"[1]

What Adams did not know was that the "animating occasion" he
longed for would come through the War for Independence. The war,
and all it entailed, would bring him great suffering. He risked his life, his
family, and his fortune. But he achieved greatness. He became the mind
behind Jefferson's Declaration and a father of his nation. He gave himself
completely to the cause of freedom and to shaping a nation under God.

He wanted. He suffered. He persevered. He deepened. He made history.

Thank God for people like John Adams.

Don't think you have to be a young person to want more. One of my
heroes is Frances Hesselbein. Frances became CEO of the Girl Scouts of the
USA in 1976 at an age when many people might be thinking about retirement. Legendary accomplishments. Reinvented the Girl Scouts. Two and
a quarter million girls, seven hundred fifty volunteers, and a staff of about
thirty thousand people. Awarded the United States of America's highest
civilian honor, the Presidential Medal of Freedom, in 1998 as a "pioneer
for women, volunteerism, diversity and opportunity."[2] The founding president of the Peter F. Drucker Institute (now Leader to Leader Institute) at
Peter Drucker's insistence.

In 2009, more than three decades after she began her leadership of
the Girl Scouts, Frances was appointed the 1951 Chair for the Study of
Leadership at the United States Military Academy at West Point. She regularly spends significant time shaping the future of the world by teaching
the young leaders there. She exposes them to other great thought leaders
she knows as well. Here she is, still shaping the future.

But here's the deal. Frances recently spoke to the leaders at the church
where I serve. Someone in our group made the mistake of asking about
her age. She took a step forward, all five feet of her, smiled, and replied,

"We never discuss age.... To retire is the language of the past.... If we are called to serve, then we know what we should be doing and, when we are done with that, there's always something else waiting." She then restated her most famous saying: "To live is to serve," and then, "If that is true, then as long as we are breathing we are serving."

Frances is not interested in a focus on the past. Her focus, even after a lifetime of service, is future, future, future.

She speaks on college campuses around the world. Students frequently ask her, "How can you stay so positive?" She looks at them and says, "Because of you!" And with great enthusiasm, she cites the volunteerism rates and the surveys that show how today's young people crave to create a better world. Frances says that there's never been a generation like this group of eighteen- to twenty-eight-year-olds, at least not since the 1930s and 1940s. And she's quick to say that the 1930s group of young people became what is commonly called the greatest generation. She should know. She was there, called to serve.

Look—I don't care if you are eighteen, thirty, or ninety. Want more! You can create a preferred future.

If you want to.

In the following pages, I want to encourage you to go after the *more* and *better* that God wants for you. I may even try to provoke you a little, if you'll let me. This world needs people who want more than nice little lives. This world needs people who care. People who want something great. People who are willing to go after it. People who would never be satisfied with anything less than a *TEN*.

The future is waiting. Let's go!

Part One

AWAKEN

Chapter 1
The Future Is in You

A REALLY COOL THING happened to me recently. I was at the ESPN Zone at Times Square for a Cotchery Foundation benefit. The Cotchery Foundation was founded by Mercedes and Jerricho Cotchery. Jerricho is a star wide receiver for the New York Jets. He and Mercedes are friends of mine, and I was at this event to support them and the causes they care about. Oh—and I'm a big football fan.

On this night, the Cotchery Foundation was raising a lot of money for several causes, but the primary beneficiary was Pride Academy Charter School. Pride Academy is located in East Orange, New Jersey. East Orange sits in the shadow of Newark and is plagued by severe problems in its educational system—problems all too common to urban America. The hope is that a successful charter school like Pride Academy will make a powerful difference in the future of many kids and the future of the community itself.

So I'm standing there in a crush of people, many of them fans who had donated in order to be there. They were given the opportunity to hang out with Jerricho, some of his teammates, and other celebrities. Lots of autographs were being signed.

A woman kind of forced her way over to me. The two beaming young girls at her side were about ten or eleven years old. "I want to meet you," she said, "and these girls said that you were the celebrity they want to meet tonight." I laughed. Politely? I thought I had been confused—again—for an old retired lineman. Big guy. Shaved head. Still eating to gain weight but not working out enough anymore. Celebrity? Ha! The last autograph I signed was the signature line of a personal check.

"No," she smiled, "we know who you are." Then the girls introduced themselves and started to thank me. They attend Pride Academy. The woman was the principal.

So what did this have to do with me?

Well, I am the senior pastor of The Life Christian Church in West Orange, New Jersey, a fairly prosperous suburb of Newark and New York City. A young woman named Rose Mary Dumenigo attends our church. Rose Mary says that she was so inspired by the message in my weekend talks that she decided—along with three other women—to create Pride Academy Charter School.

Rose Mary was a schoolteacher in Newark. She was pouring her life into kids, as do most teachers, but felt stuck in a system that didn't work. She wanted more. She heard me say—over and over—that we have the God-given ability to create new realities. She believed me. She started a school. Kids' lives are being saved.

Enter Jerricho and Mercedes Cotchery. In one of our weekend celebrations, Mercedes experienced a presentation about a serving opportunity at Pride Academy. She was inspired to get involved. She started RESH 180, a mentoring program where she teaches the students values that provide the foundation for life success. She has rallied many other volunteers to serve at Pride Academy. The Cotchery Foundation has raised a lot of money to help this school succeed.

And I got to be a celebrity—at least in the minds of two beautiful kids—for about sixty seconds.

But that's not the point. The point is that I've had a lot of people, though usually in less dramatic ways, tell me that the message they hear me share again and again and again has changed their lives and the lives of people around them.

What is that message? Well...here it is. I hope it impacts your life too.

The future is in you now.

Most of us have some awareness of the future that is in us. We have moments when we catch our breath in wonder as we briefly glimpse possibilities vastly preferred over our past and present. We intuit something great and grand and from God percolating just beneath the surface of our lives.

We can become fully awake to this future. We can bring this future from the nebulous realm of the subconscious into the world of the conscious. We can move the mystery toward the intentional. Once we do, we can partner with God to create the tomorrow He has dreamed for us—the future we were made for. We can create our God-inspired futures.

God-inspired futures are futures that are better, best, preferred. But God does not force these futures on us. He allows us to choose whether to actualize them. We can cooperate with Him in the continuing act of creating the life and the world He envisioned. And we can experience more and more what He made in the beginning, before terrible human choices messed everything up.

I want this preferred future God planned for each of us and for those we love. I'm not only referring to future generations—opportunities that only our children or even their children will be able to experience. I am talking about imminent futures, eventualities that we can all witness sooner rather than later.

I want to help you conceive and birth the futures—yours and others'— that are gestating in you but are yet unborn. Countless lives are waiting to be changed. There are always new futures waiting to live.

Dr. Thomas P. Barnett, former advisor to the Office of the Secretary of Defense of the United States, was tasked with the burdensome responsibility of studying the future of the world. He writes about the need "to imagine a future worth creating" and to "actually try to build it."[1] He says, "I choose to see it as a moral responsibility—a duty to leave our children a better world."[2]

If someone has the ability to imagine a better future and holds the power to create it, then he or she is morally responsible to do just that. We all have facing us incredible potentialities that can cause an entire new reality to exist. When we consider these possibilities, common and moral sense should direct us toward purposeful action.

We must take the actions necessary to bring about the promptings in our hearts. In the New Testament, James talks about the worthlessness of knowing the good we ought to do and not doing it. He says it is a sin (Jas. 4:17). If opportunities lie dormant in our minds and are never actualized, we are living inferior lives. Purposeful inaction is a detriment to the future of our world.

Donald Miller wrote a beautiful book about how to write a better story with our lives. He said, "A character who wants something and overcomes conflict to get it is the basic structure of a good story."[3] Profound. I think "living a good story" is a loaded proposition. One part of "good" is "interesting." We should live interesting stories. The more important part of "good" is "moral." It is not enough to live an interesting story; there must be a moral to our story. What great story does not have a moral conflict?

Who can say what is moral? What authority determines what is good? I am a Christian. My understanding of morality is premised on the Judeo-Christian worldview. Whether or not your worldview is the same as mine, I think we can agree that there is a difference between right and wrong, good and evil. And I hope you'll keep reading. Whether you are a Christ follower or not, I hope that we can agree that we can create a "good" future together.

Anyone who thinks one thing should be done rather than another has acknowledged a "moral ought." Keep the law. Help the poor. Save the trees. This "ought to" is rooted in the idea that better, best, and preferred must be practiced in a moral context.

There has been a common understanding of morality throughout time even though it has been expressed uniquely through various cultures at various times. I believe, as do other people of faith, that this implies the existence of a moral lawgiver: God—the Creator of conscience. He gave us the ability to discern right and wrong.

And I believe that the future we are responsible to create must be pursued with the idea of what's right and what's good deeply impressed in our minds. This guarantees that our stories will be filled with moral conflict. Good.

One of the greatest moral conflicts in American history was the struggle for the abolition of slavery. William Seward was a New York state senator (1830–1834), state governor (1838–1842), and the leading candidate in the Republican Party for the 1860 presidential nomination. He was defeated by the relatively unknown Abraham Lincoln. Seward, however, decided to continue serving his country during a time of tremendous moral crisis by accepting President Lincoln's invitation to become secretary of state.

During his earlier years as a United States senator, Seward set a moral momentum toward ending slavery by advocating an allegiance to "higher law." He acknowledged that some believed that the United States Constitution permitted, or perhaps ignored, slavery. In a famous speech to the Senate, Seward said, "But there is a higher law than the Constitution." He then made a future-changing argument, based on moral law, against the inglorious institution of slavery.[4]

President Lincoln was influenced mightily by Seward's concept of a higher, moral law. He coupled that philosophy with his own strong conviction that the basis of American independence—that all men are created equal—came directly from God Himself. The argument against slavery was essentially a moral argument for a better future for a nation and its people. This concept was anchored in God's mandate for the equality of every human being, a partial motive for the Civil War, which won freedom for millions of formerly enslaved people and their progeny.

When Richmond, Virginia, the capital of the Confederate States of America, fell to Union forces on April 3, 1865, Lincoln and his entourage showed up the next day. They walked dangerously through the streets of the city—now golden streets—echoing the voice of freedom as throngs of newly freed slaves flocked the vicinity of the defeated capital. The emancipated surrounded the Great Emancipator with such force and determination that the soldiers guarding him were helpless in keeping them at a safe distance. With great passion, this group sang the president's praises, hailing him as their Messiah, shouting, "Glory, hallelujah!"

Lincoln knew better than to accept such acclamation. He responded, "Don't kneel to me; that is not right. You must kneel to God only, and thank him for the liberty you will hereafter enjoy."[5] While Lincoln was used as an instrument to unfold the preferred futures of people who had never tasted the fruits of freedom, he knew that this better future came from God, the highest law.

So, the future is in us.

And not just any future. It is the future that God has planned for us and our world.

We are responsible to bring this future out of the realm of the unseen and into the world of the seen and lived.

And we can. We can create a better future for ourselves and others.

If we really want to.

Chapter 2

High Hope Levels

WE CAN VIEW HISTORY through the lens of at least three fundamental philosophies: pessimism, optimism, or pessimistic optimism. Those who have a pessimistic view of history obsess over the failure of humanity. They believe that because human beings are so messed up, history will eventually spiral down into tremendous failure. Pessimists are the folks we see parading through the streets of our major metropolitan cities, like Manhattan, carrying signs for various causes that read something like, "The end is coming!" and offering no hope of escape from our fated extinction.

The other end of the spectrum is called optimism and it focuses strictly on human potential. This philosophy surmises that human beings alone have the ability to fashion a better world. Karl Marx, for instance, subscribed to this humanistic view. We have seen the demise of one of its offspring, communism, in our lifetime. Can't we agree that none of us are able to sort our way through the multitude of problems and unfortunate realities in this world just by human power alone?

In the middle of these two extremes, however, comes a balanced and biblical view—pessimistic optimism. This system of thought recognizes that the world and human beings really are messed up, but because God is involved in history, there is every reason to believe that things can be better. Sometimes, however, it's difficult to have hope.

On September 12, 2001, I spent a night serving as a chaplain in the ruins of the World Trade Center in downtown Manhattan. Man, did I see some horrific stuff. People were frantically looking for loved ones. I saw courageous aid workers alerted by rescue canines that something human was in a section of rubble, and I watched them furiously work in the hope of finding someone buried alive. Instead, they found only a body part. I spent time at the makeshift morgue where there was dark surprise that so few bodies were found. And I saw the widespread disappointment grow at the realization that virtually no one was alive to be rescued. I had the thoughts most people in the world did as they watched the story unfold: *How can there be such evil in the world? How can there be such pain and loss and grief?*

While walking through the devastation, I found a tanker truck from the West Orange fire department manned by a group of dedicated firefighters. They were working hard, trying to put out some of the smoldering fires as well as digging through the rubble looking for survivors. Just a few weeks before, I had been asked to help dedicate a new fire truck in town. The mayor had smashed a bottle of champagne to christen the vehicle, and I prayed. I was also asked to pray for several new firefighters who were inducted that day, including the first female firefighter in the history of West Orange.

Well, in the middle of that 9/11 devastation, here stood that young woman. One of her first experiences as a firefighter. I wanted to somehow encourage her and those other courageous souls as they fought through one of the most terrible events in recent history.

I didn't know what to say.

So I simply asked, "Would you mind if we prayed?" The quickness with which they formed a circle and joined hands was revealing. We felt the presence of God in the middle of that destruction, in the buildings destroyed by evil. There was hope. I didn't fully understand it, and I imagine those firefighters didn't either. But there was hope.

I am reminded of the marvelous Bible story where Jesus was walking on the water toward his disciples during a tremendous storm. These men, huddled in a boat far from shore, tossed about by perilous waves, were overwhelmed by fear. And then they were sucker-punched with a double dose of distress by what they thought was a ghost—Jesus walking on the water. The closer the image of Christ appeared to them, the more alarmed they became. Jesus calmed their fears by simply saying, "I am here. Don't be afraid." In the midst of their trouble, he showed up and said, "It's me. I am real. And I am here. Don't be afraid." (See John 6:16–21.)

Because of the presence of God in our world, there is reason to hope. Humanity is in somewhat of a mess, but things can get better. God intends for them to get better. Because of His active participation in our lives and in our world, we can believe that good will defeat evil, love will conquer hate, hope will crush despair, and, ultimately, that we will be led to a better future.

I recently read an academic paper that states, "According to the literature, the development of high levels of hope is necessary to be an effective leader."[1] I like that. What we need are high hope levels. All is not lost.

You will overflow with confident hope through the power of the Holy Spirit.

—Rom. 15:13, NLT

For preferred futures to leave the realm of mind and spirit and become physical and practical, we must practice leadership. In some instances, this may only be leadership of the self. We must lead ourselves to turn an idea into a reality, the potential into the actual. The kind of futures that

I advocate, however, are most often completely realized only by leading others.

Leaders accept responsibility for others. The kind of preferred futures we can build must involve more than just ourselves. We should be bringing others, many others, into the realization of the dreams that exist in our minds and in their minds. Leaders do not just experience. They help others experience. They do not just do. They help others do. And they do not only create for themselves. They empower others to create as well.

One way to refer to the kind of leadership that actively cares about creating a better world for oneself and others is *moral leadership.*

I am currently coaching a businessman who owns a telecommunications company. He gets fired up with volunteering for nonprofit organizations and giving money away to various charities. While his business was profitable and generally running well, the field of telecommunications didn't particularly excite him. We decided to craft a mission statement for his business that would link his moral energies with running a successful company:

> Our mission is to be a model business that honors God and serves people by operating according to the highest values in achieving profitability in order to practice generosity toward our customers, our employees, communities, and worthy charitable organizations.

After we finalized this mission statement, his whole demeanor changed from frustrated apathy to exultant animation. He understood his mission to be a moral mission that would erect preferred futures for not only the company as a whole, but also for his "customers, employees, communities, and...charitable organizations." Now we were talking about hundreds, maybe thousands, of lives that could be transformed as a result of this firm's success. This business concept and motivation existed in his heart. But now he was able to successfully connect and submit his business to a higher law, a bigger picture, and exactly what he felt God had wired him to do.

He had in him the ability to create whatever kind of company he purposed, but he just hadn't realized it. He thought he was married to the mundane business of only making money, providing for his family, keeping his promises, and being a good citizen.

If you have the desire to form your own company, what kind of company would you build? How would it satisfy your higher motivations and flow from higher law? How would it positively impact the lives of others? Would it be "good"? Would it be better than present reality? Would it be the kind of company that God could bless? These are the kinds of questions that moral leaders ask.

There is higher stuff that can catapult us from basic life mode into a reality that is far more remarkable than what we may feel stuck with. We do not have to react; we can proact. We can decide to create God-inspired futures for ourselves and for others.

Intellectual strategies alone will not motivate people. Only a company with a real mission or a sense of purpose that comes out of an intuitive or spiritual dimension will capture people's hearts. And you must have people's hearts to inspire the hard work required to realize a vision.

—John Naisbitt and Patricia Aburdene,
Reinventing the Corporation[1]

In this era of self-development, we have an unlimited number of resources to transform ourselves into happier and healthier people. Through self-help resources, worrywarts can be cured, procrastinators can be reformed, and overweight people can become thin by learning to eat like the French or by giving carbs the boot. Unfortunately, the self-help movement seems to begin and end there—self. You and me, singular human beings.

While there is everything right with becoming emotionally and physically healthier, there is something morally wrong if we are our sole focus in life. We must focus on "others-help" versus "self-help." It's not only about us.

This is not another self-centered, quick-gratification, what-I-want-and-need, me-me-me, mine-mine-mine book. This is why I connect the incredible possibility of creating things that are superior to what presently exists to the exponential power of leadership. Regardless of who you are or what your natural inclinations or giftings are, you can and must lead yourself and others to the best possible reality. If there is a better future out there in a world full of possibility, I refuse to experience it alone. I want to influence others to experience it with me.

There is a promise that you will live a more fulfilling life when you are involved in the ongoing creative activity of God. When we lose our lives in His life, when we lose ourselves in something bigger than ourselves, then we really find life at its best.

When life is at its best, your relationships are more fulfilling. Your food tastes better. You enjoy your exercise routines more. The sun shines brighter. The ocean is bluer. The air is more refreshing.

I'm writing this on a lovely spring evening, sitting on my deck and watching my beautiful wife of twenty-eight years grilling pork chops, which our family will be sharing at dinner in a few minutes. I'm joyfully content. Life is good.

But that goodness doesn't come simply from watching the movement of a pretty woman preparing a mouth-watering meal. It comes from experiencing this moment in the context of a life that's inspired by a good God.

Chapter 3

The Role You Were Made For

"How great is man! We think, and through our bodies the reality flows out into the external world. We do not create out of nothing, as God creates, but in the sense of which we are speaking here it is proper to say that the artist does create and each of us creates.... When I create, I bring forth in the external universe that he has created. But nevertheless, understanding the limitations and differences, it is perfectly proper to say God creates, and we create.

—Francis A. Schaeffer,
True Spirituality[1]

FOR OUR WEDDING ANNIVERSARY, my wife and I were given tickets to the Broadway show *The Lion King*. I was weary from a long and intense week—frankly a little bit bored. I dozed off and on through the first few scenes. Then one particular scene, rife with powerful significance, grabbed and held my attention for the rest of the musical.

Loosely based on Shakespeare's *Hamlet*, the story begins in the kingdom of Pride Lands with a grand celebration honoring Simba, the newborn son of the lion king Mufasa and heir to the throne. Scar, Mufasa's brother, is enraged. He schemes to murder his brother and nephew, seizing what he believes is his rightful position as king. Only Mufasa is killed, but Simba is falsely led to believe, by his uncle's selfish manipulations, that he is at fault for his father's death. Out of guilt, shame, and fear from Scar's wrath, the young cub flees from the kingdom and Scar is crowned king. As would be expected during the reign of an immoral and ruthless leader, Pride Lands takes a dramatic turn for the worse. It metamorphoses from a place of freedom, peace, and plenty into a barren wasteland decimated by evil and hopelessness.

Years later as a young adult, Simba is compelled to return to Pride Lands—the place of his destiny—to overthrow the ruthless dictator, reclaim his royal position, and bring healing and restoration. While his lack of confidence and hesitation is evident, Simba is encouraged by a sage named Rafiki who claims Mufasa is "alive" and demands Simba to look inside himself and recognize his father's presence.

> "I know your father," says Rafiki.
>
> "My father is dead," answers Simba.
>
> "Nope! He's alive. I'll show him to you." Rafiki leads Simba to a pool of clear water. "Look down there."
>
> First Simba sees his own reflection, then the face of his father.
>
> "You see, he lives in you!" says Rafiki.
>
> Simba hears a familiar voice call his name. He looks up. His father's ghostlike image appears among the stars.
>
> "Look inside yourself," says the apparition. "You must take your place in the circle of life. Remember who you are…"
>
> The vision fades.

I realize that this is a fictitious, humanistic story famous for thrilling children with its fantastic characters and enchanting plot. Yet this one scene gripped my thoughts with its analogy to potent spiritual truths—the dire need for every one of us to know who we are through our Father and to accept our destined place in this world to create better, best, and preferred futures. Our "circle of life" has to do with finding our place of possibility and accountability in this world. If we do not play our God-designed roles here, there are a multitude of futures that will never happen.

Every human being is born with the incredible capacity to impact his world, regardless of how bad things may seem or how helpless a person may feel. How do I know this? Because we were created in the image and glory of God (1 Cor. 11:7). Most of us see different faces when we look in mirrors. Some may see a loser, a victim, or someone alienated from his destiny. People of faith recognize that this God-image was marred and our world terribly wounded when the first human beings chose to live their way instead of God's way. But when we look into a mirror, as children of God, we should see the image of our Father reflected back. Biblical scholar W. E. Vines reminds us that "the condition of man as a fallen creature has not entirely effaced the 'image'; he is still suitable to bear responsibility, he still has God-like qualities, such as love of goodness and beauty, none of which are found in a mere animal."[2]

Every human being is created with tremendous potential to do good. Though we are also born with the potential to do evil (Ps. 51:5), when we believe in Jesus (John 3:7) we enter another dimension of purpose, privilege, and power: "To all who received him, to those who believed in his name, he gave the right to become the children of God" (John 1:12). Through this spiritual birth, we are relationally reconnected to God our Father and His image in us is reconstructed. We are partakers of a new, divine nature (2 Pet. 1:4). Though we are still capable of doing wrong, our basic instinct now is to do good: "Each of you is now a new person. You are becoming more and more like your Creator" (Col. 3:10 CEV).

The Lion King's tagline reads, "Life's greatest adventure is finding your place in the Circle of Life." From the time Simba is a young cub, his father teaches him that one day he will assume his place as the king of Pride Lands. Simba, however, is not to approach his calling without a deep sense of responsibility. He must play the role for which he was chosen. If not, Simba's world is lost.

Similar to Simba's fictional responsibility, we are mandated to assume our own positions in this world—to take our place in the circle of life—bearing God's image and using our God-given authority to bring help and hope into a broken world: "Death ruled like a king because Adam had sinned. But that cannot compare with what Jesus Christ has done. God has been so kind to us, and he has accepted us because of Jesus. And so we will live and rule like kings" (Rom. 5:17, CEV). We are called to "reign in life" (NIV).

Do you know who you are? Are you ruling in life? Or do you live as if you are hopelessly subjected to all the negative forces in your world, left powerless to make a difference?

Look in the mirror! What do you see? Excuses? Limitations? A damaged past? Lack of talents? What you should see is the image of your heavenly Father (Gen. 1:26–27). The one who has crowned you with the authority to rule in this life. The one who is calling you to take your necessary place. You must not run from your destiny.

I love the sequence in *It's a Wonderful Life* when George (played by Jimmy Stewart) is shown what the world would be like if he had not lived. He saw a life that wouldn't have been saved, love that wouldn't have been given, children that wouldn't have been born, a business that wouldn't have been built, and people who wouldn't have been helped as a result.

What kind of world will we have if we don't play the roles we were made to play? What futures deficit will exist? What love lost? What potential thwarted? What business not built? What book not written? Church not started? Movie not made? Project not funded? Because we didn't do what we were made to do.

Chapter 4

Created to Transcend

So God created man in His own image; in the image of God He created him; male and female He created them. Then God blessed them, and God said to them, "...fill the earth and subdue it; have dominion over...every living thing that moves on the earth."

—Genesis 1:27, 28, NKJV

JAMES SIRE WRITES THAT human beings are "created in the image of God and thus possess personality, self-transcendence, intelligence, morality, gregariousness, and creativity."[1] Because we are like God, we share many of his attributes, though in limited ways. In order to see the characteristics that are stamped in the heart of every human being, we only have to take a look at God. We have personality, or self-consciousness; we are conscious of ourselves and have the ability to make our own decisions. We have intelligence; we are born with the ability to think. We have morality, the aptitude to discern good from evil. Moreover, we are gregarious, or social, beings.

I want to focus on the other two characteristics Sire mentions—self-transcendence and creativity. They provide the foundation for the privilege and responsibility of causing preferred futures. God specifically wired us to transcend and affect present realities and to create realities that do not yet exist.

All human beings are born with self-transcendence—the ability to rise above temporal circumstances in order to influence their environment. By environment, I don't mean Earth Day stuff—recycling, saving whales, or driving hybrid cars—although we must steward our physical environment. What I'm talking about is this: we have the inborn power to influence the environments of our lives and others' lives, to change the way things are, and, ultimately, to cause preferred futures to come into existence.

If we could draw a circle around everything that exists, we would see God outside of the circle. He is independent of and completely unconstrained by his environment. He can make decisions and act toward whatever is in that circle. He has transcendence. Most of us instinctively understand this concept. What many of us do not understand, however, is that part of being created in God's image means that we have self-transcendence.

While God's transcendence is constrained only by His character, meaning He can only will and act in ways that come from His infinitely good nature, our transcendence, of course, is limited to a much greater degree. Many things happen in our world we can't control. However, if you were able to draw a circle around everything that you can manage, make decisions about, or impress upon in a meaningful way, you would probably be surprised how large that circle could be. There would certainly be many, if not most, things concerning your "self." In fact, part of the evidence of God's Spirit impacting our lives is the concept of self-control. The Bible teaches us that "the fruit of the Spirit is…self-control" (Gal. 5:22–23, NKJV). We can resolve what to do or what not to do about ourselves, and we can act accordingly. We have transcendence. - *The ability to go beyond ordinary limits, surpassing, exceeding*

There are many things we cannot change. You cannot individually manipulate the global economy or whether your husband dies from a heart attack or being born with only seven fingers. For example, each of us is born with genetics predisposing us to certain medical conditions, bone structure, or eye color. We cannot, with our thoughts, add one inch to our height. I have also sadly learned that regardless of effort, we cannot add any significant hair follicles to a head predetermined to male-pattern baldness. But even concerning these outside-our-circle-of-control things, we can still practice what I call *reactive transcendence:* We can choose how to respond to negative life realities.

In his chilling account of years in concentration camps, leading to his renowned theories in psychiatry, Viktor Frankl wrote about his search to find a reason to live during this horrific time. The book, *Man's Search for Meaning*, explores his epiphany that although he could not change the fact that he was in a concentration camp, he had the capacity to control how he responded to the situation. He could feel hate or love. He could have a sense of purpose or remain hopeless. It was his choice. Even in these terrible circumstances, Frankl exercised his power to transcend, to rise above. Further, he did impact outcomes, particularly concerning his own life, by choosing to live when his comrades had given up. While younger, healthier men around him were dying tragically, he determined to nurture his own sense of purpose. Frankl quoted, of all people, Nietzsche: "He who has a *why* to live for can bear with any *how*."[2] Frankl practiced reactive transcendence.

While Frankl's example falls on a grander scale of reactive transcendence, let's look at this from a more applicable perspective. We may not have been blessed with supersonic metabolism, but we can make lifestyle choices to maintain a healthy body weight—we can exercise regularly and eat better foods. We may not have been born with a silver spoon and may now have what appears to be a limited income, but we can multiply financial opportunities by spending less, saving more, and investing wisely. Regardless of our present circumstances, we can make appropriate choices to better our lives and our futures.

Giving rise to preferred futures happens mostly, though, in the realm of *proactive transcendence.* The multitude of things we can purpose. Impact. Change. Now. The profoundly wise "Serenity Prayer," popularized by the Twelve-Step movement, echoes both reactive and proactive transcendence.

God, grant me the serenity to accept the things I cannot change;
The courage to change the things I can, and
The wisdom to know the difference.

I think many of us focus our attention on "the things I *cannot* change" part of this prayer. Shouldn't we also fervently plug into "the things we *can* change" part? Shouldn't we practice proactive transcendence? One of the greatest disgraces in life is when we accept the things to which we should take exception. We should be asking ourselves, "What *can* I do?" "How *can* I make a difference?" "Where *can* I be an influence?"

Theologians say that God is both transcendent and immanent; He is out there and He shows up here. God decided to get involved in the world over which He had transcendence. This is the nature of God. For God so loved the world he sent His Son, Jesus Christ, to heal and restore humanity's brokenness (John 3:16). God "became flesh and lived among us" (John 1:14, NCV).

Just as He shows up, we need to show up. We must see our potential to transcend—like God did and does—to make decisions, to act, to change things.

Each of us must find areas in our world to draw a circle around—where we can say, "There . . . I can make a difference . . . *there.*"

The Reverend Doctor Wilson Goode drew a circle around children who have an incarcerated parent. Dr. Goode, a Baptist minister, was the first African American mayor of Philadelphia. He served for two terms. Then he was appointed deputy assistant secretary of education by President Clinton. In spite of his historic personal success, he became more and more aware and concerned that generations of young people were in a crisis that threatened their futures, their families and communities, and our entire society. Incredible numbers of the children of incarcerated people were following their parents into prison.

Dr. Goode tells a heartrending story of a prison which houses a man, his son, and his grandson. The grandson never met his grandfather—until they met in prison. Wilson Goode decided to be more than heartbroken, though. He decided to draw a circle around this devastating problem. Then to enter it. And to change it. He chose to practice proactive transcendence.

So, in 2000, he left the comfort and status of the Department of Education and founded a nonprofit called Amachi. Amachi is a partnership of secular and faith-based organizations working together to identify children of prisoners to match them with caring adults. Now 359 agencies serve 300,000 children all across the United States!

Amachi is a Nigerian word that means "who knows what God has brought through this child."

I was with Dr. Goode one day when a young man who was leading a community nonprofit came asking the great man for advice. The first thing Mayor Goode told him—with great passion—was that most nonprofits try to do too many things: "Figure out your mission and do that. Period. Amachi exists to mentor young people whose parents are incarcerated. That's it."

We are not God. We can't practice transcendence over everything and maybe not even many things. But each of us can find something to draw a circle around and say, "I can change that." Dr Goode is involved in many important causes. But he drew a circle around this one. And the future will be different because he did.

It amazes me how passively many people of faith live—as if we have no control over anything, no ability to make even the slightest difference.

One reason for this is that many are unknowingly fatalistic in their world-view. Fatalism is the opposite of faith.

Buddha summarized his views in *The Four Noble Truths*. The first of these four statements reads, "Life is suffering." Vishal Mangalwadi—a well-known author, lecturer, and development worker in India—has been frustrated that many people in Third World countries have adopted this worldview and mantra, which he believes has promoted a cycle of poverty.

Mangalwadi says, "Life need not be suffering. A great deal of suffering is avoidable if we know what life is and how it ought to be lived."[3] It is his experience that many people who have embraced these ideas are taught to accept suffering and manage it by practicing some form of meditation or other means of spiritual escapism. Folks spend an enormous amount of time and energy trying to achieve nirvana instead of drawing a circle around suffering and taking action to make things better. We must care enough, believe enough, and risk enough to alleviate suffering where possible.

A fatalistic worldview also explains how someone like Osho—a spiritual guru and founder of his own commune in Oregon—would write in his book *God is Dead*, "If God is a reality, then man is a slave, a puppet. All the strings are in his hands, even your life. He pulls the strings, you dance; he pulls the strings, you cry; he pulls the strings, you start murders, suicide, war. You are just a puppet and he is the puppeteer."[4]

Many of us do live as if God is the master puppeteer and we are his mindless puppets. How sad. And how wrong. God gave us the ability to do or not to do. Right now, touch your forehead. Touch your arm. Who did this? God? No, you did. Many of us falsely assume that every time we reach our arms out to do anything, God moved them for us. Absolutely not! God gives us the ability to move our arms. God willed that we can will. The Bible affirms this: "For it is God who works in you to will and to act according to his good purpose" (Phil. 2:13)!

Ask yourself: What am I waiting for? How can I get involved in what God is doing in the world now? "We are God's workmanship, created in Christ Jesus to do good works, which God prepared in advance for us to do" (Eph. 2:10). As people of faith, we were not created to be passive, small-brained, tiny-hearted believers. We must view life expansively. We must draw big circles around large areas of potential impact. We were made to make a difference.

Chapter 5

Created to Create

Every human being…has a will, or will power. It is our inclination and capacity to act on our own and to produce what we find to be good—to be freely creative.

—Dallas Willard,
The Divine Conspiracy[1]

WHEN I THINK OF transcendence, I think of the ability

- to choose,
- to respond, and
- to change things that already are.

Creativity is a step beyond this. It allows us to create things that are not yet. Out of the mind of a human being can come an idea that, when materialized, brings an entirely new reality into existence.

Philosopher and theologian Dallas Willard writes about this kinship between idea and actuality in *The Divine Conspiracy*. Willard writes that if you are seated in a room, probably everything you see owes its existence to the ideas of one or more persons. When you look up into the sky and see an airplane, you are looking at an idea that began in an individual's mind and was willed into physicality. Think about this. When the Wright Brothers imagined and then created the first flying machine in 1903, they caused a plethora of new realities to come into being.

Today, these include an aviation industry that operates over two million flights a month, flies about thirty-five million hours a year, supports approximately fifteen thousand airports worldwide, and employs hundreds of thousands of people.

We have entire economies that revolve around the airline industry. These expanding worlds were all birthed from an idea.

God, when he created us in His image, instilled in our own being the open-ended opportunity to give birth to new futures. Stan Hickman, an African American criminal defense attorney, came to me recently with an idea. He conveyed his desire to start a program designed specifically for at-risk black young men. Over the course of his career, Stan noticed an alarming growth of clientele between the ages of fifteen and eighteen. Not only did he find more and more teenagers entrenched in the criminal justice system, but their crimes were becoming exponentially more severe. This attorney proposed a program of mentoring and roundtable discussions between troubled young men and a panel of strong leaders in the community, such as police officers, entrepreneurs, judges, and educators. He hopes to target these young people by exploring and offering them positive alternatives for a better future.

Instead of being another statistic that gets lost in society, each of these young men will be able to recognize a new and better life. Instead of going to jail, a young man will be going to college, starting a business, and influencing the lives of future employees. Instead of overdosing on heroin, a young man will get married, start a family, and create a better life for his children—children that will never be born unless their father's life is saved now.

All of these futures exponentially impact thousands more futures. Stan has in him the futures of potentially thousands of people.

We are all called to work in the "futures" business! We must understand the implications of this truth—each and every one of us has a multiplicity of futures inside of us. Futures that will not occur unless we create them. Futures for which we are accountable.

Stan believes that his idea is a God-inspired idea. But Stan has a choice. He can opt whether or not to bring this into reality. It's this simple: It can and will come to pass if he cooperates with God in its creation. But if he refuses, those futures will be aborted.

There are so many things inside us. We often believe the only way they'll get out is by watching God wave a magic wand to make things happen. God did not create human beings as thoughtless robots, but as partners with Him in continued creation.

Take a moment. Reflect on your participation in God's creative activity. Look down the road thirty, forty, fifty years. What futures exist because of you? What futures are inside you at this very moment? What sort of ideas do you have brewing in your mind that can significantly contribute to the worlds of business, politics, or social reform?

Rembrandt could have decided whether or not to paint. Bach could have decided whether or not to write and play music. Do you have a book in you that needs to be written? Do you have a philanthropic idea that you can't keep inside any more? Do you have a ministry you just must give birth to? What is inside you, shouting to get out into reality? We all have the capacity to determine futures.

Ludwig van Beethoven understood the call to birth his internal ideas into the artistic realities that made him a musical icon. In 1802, when he was thirty-one years old, Beethoven journaled some thoughts now referred to as the *Heiligenstadt Testament*. He was experiencing the onset of deafness, which would grow progressively worse until he would be totally unable to hear. Beethoven wrote of his relentless struggle with depression and suicidal thoughts as a result of this calamity. In his lament, however, he concluded: "It seemed impossible to depart this world until I had brought forth all the things I felt inspired to create." His music was one reason that caused him to live.

What are you so desperate to create that it motivates you to live?

We each have things inside us that will not exist unless we create them. All of these are ideas in the world of spirit; they do not physically exist. You were created to create them.

> Creation left to itself is incomplete, and humans are called to be co-creators with God, bringing forth the potentialities the creator has hidden. Creation is full of secrets waiting to be discovered, riddles which human intelligence is expected to unlock.
>
> —Michael Novak,
> *The Spirit of Democratic Capitalism*[2]

We participate in God's continued creative activity in our world, whether in the conception of a child, designing a piece of art, developing a business, writing a curriculum for learning groups, or imagining new inventions. All of the things that we create point to the Creator and reflect His beauty: "Instinctively we do know that true beauty proceeds only from Deity."[3]

We are made in God's image, created to create beautiful, new realities. The birth of a child is a wonderful analogy. Who is the creator? God! But that child would not be conceived except by the will and action of its parents—a man and a woman. In the presence of a newborn baby, we do not think about the act of conceiving. We feel a sense of awe, appreciating the wonder and beauty of a newly birthed life. We think about God, through whom each of us is fearfully and wonderfully made.

When we create a beautiful thing, we bring something into the world of the material. Somehow we understand its origin is in the spiritual world, and we instinctively give God the glory: "So we fix our eyes not on what is seen, but on what is unseen. For what is seen is temporary, but what is unseen is eternal" (2 Cor. 4:18).

You do not have to accept ugliness, whether in a landscape or a marriage or a community. You have the potential to will and act to make something beautiful that reflects God's grandeur instead of humanity's mess. You can bring change into your world in such a way that people catch their breath and marvel when they see something of God in what you have done.

I know the obvious instinct is to think about reflecting beauty in terms of art. But what is art, specifically, to you? It may be an idea for a business that creates a wonderful environment for people to work in. Or perhaps it's an idea that, when developed, simply enhances and adds pleasure to people's lives. Or an educational program that helps kids learn in a revolutionary new way. We can create beautiful things in so many areas of life that can bring meaning and joy.

In Exodus 31, God says, "Look, I have chosen Bezalel....I have filled him with the Spirit of God, giving him great wisdom, intelligence and skill in all kinds of crafts. He is able to create beautiful objects from gold, silver, and bronze. He is skilled in cutting and setting gemstones and in carving wood. He is a master at every craft!" (Ex. 31:2–5, NLT). God was saying that He intended to use this man to create marvelous things that would be used in God's service. What has He chosen you to create? Why has He given you great wisdom, intelligence, and skill? There are creative purposes for which you have been filled with the Spirit of God! Your destiny awaits you.

Look in the mirror. Remember who you are. God wants to use you to bring His beauty into our world. You were made for this!

Part One

Reflection Questions

1. Consider John 10:10, where Jesus said, "I came to give life—life in all its fullness" (NCV) or "more and better life than [you] ever dreamed of" (MSG). Using this Scripture verse as your guide, how would you rate your life on a scale of one to *TEN*?

2. Explore the moral obligation to become your best self and to help others become their best selves. How could creating your best future be connected to creating the best futures of others? Describe the fulfillment you will experience when you create a better future for yourself and those around you.

3. What are some areas in your life or in the world around you in which you practice "reactive transcendence" (accepting those things you cannot change)? When should you practice "proactive transcendence" (changing those things that you can change)?

4. What are some things that you should draw a circle around and say, "I can change that"? Think first about things concerning yourself. Next, think about things in the world around you.

5. What futures—yours and others—are gestating in you? If you had the ability to create something beautiful that doesn't presently exist, what beautiful reality would you create?

Part Two

DISCOVER

Chapter 6

Naming Possibility

It is a dangerous business to arrive in eternity with possibilities which one himself has prevented from becoming actualities. Possibility is a hint from God. A person must follow it. If God does not want it, then let Him hinder it. The person must not hinder it himself.

—Soren Kierkegaard,
from *The Journals of Kierkegaard*, 1848

THIS STATEMENT FROM KIERKEGAARD, the great Danish philosopher and theologian, has powerfully influenced my worldview. I have long been fascinated with the tension between God's predetermined purposes and a human being's free will. God clearly designed a destiny for each of us. But it seems just as clear to me that He offers us choices within His predestination that are, to a large degree, determinative. What we believe makes a difference. How we pray makes a difference. What we decide makes a difference. What we do makes a difference. Our choices regulate whether or not we can experience all the potentialities that God has destined for us.

Think about the way God related to the very first human beings. He created a world of possibility for Adam and Eve but gave them the ability to choose whether or not to live the lives He had purposed for them. They had to exercise their will in order to bring to pass what God had dreamed for both of them and, interestingly enough, Himself. Lives imbued with God's presence and promise, experienced in an earthly paradise, would have been theirs had they agreed to God's way instead of rebelliously choosing their own.

Philip Yancey writes:

> Genesis tells of God's final set of choices. . . . Man and woman came into being. . . . Alone of all God's creatures, they had a moral capacity to rebel against their creator. The sculptures could spit at the sculptor; the characters in the play could rewrite the lines. They were, in a word, free.
>
> "Man is God's risk," said one theologian. . . . Nearly everything theologians say about human freedom sounds somehow right and somehow wrong. How can a sovereign God take risks or imprison himself? Yet God's creation of man and woman approached that kind of astonishing self-limitation.[1]

Adam and Eve's first and greatest choice was whether or not to accept God's plan to live and rule in the garden from which they could have expanded God's beauty to the entire earth. Within that context, there are examples of how God relates to every member of the human family in ways great and small. One of my favorites is this: "Now the LORD God had formed out of the ground all the beasts of the field and all the birds of the air. He brought them to the man to see what he would name them; and whatever the man called each living creature, that was its name" (Gen. 2:19).

God, in His infinite wisdom, created the world in intricate measure and form. He was exact in every minute detail—from the specific rotation of the earth on its axis to the precise measure of sunlight necessary to make a daisy grow. But into this perfection, He introduced a variable: people—to whom He gave the capacity to make decisions, even about the perfect things He had made.

"Adam, look at what I created. Whatever you decide to call it, that's what its name will be."

Don't you see God operating that way in our lives? He creates something, or has an idea. He brings it to a person, and says, "Look what I have for you. What do you want to do with it? What do you want to name this? Whatever you name it, that's what its name will be. It's up to you." It seems that God is constantly alternating between being a spectator and being a participant in human affairs. This much I know: God insists that we participate in bringing even what He says is possible to pass. At very distinct times in my life, it seems that God has brought His dreams for me, and His dreams for the areas over which I have influence, and said, "Terry, this is what I have made for you. I call this possible. Now what do you want to call it?"

Possibilities are hints from God! They enter our consciousness through the portal of spirit and become a vision, a thought, an idea. We must pray, make decisions, activate faith, and take action in order for these things to leave the spiritual and become physically real. God wants us to join with Him in crafting our preferred futures.

We partner with God in destiny fulfillment. Eugene Peterson wrote that we pray in the *middle voice*—the space between active and passive.[2] He uses this terminology from the discipline of grammar to describe how we partner with God through prayer. I believe that we also live in the middle voice. We do not live in the active voice, singularly causing and bringing things into existence, because God is the primary causer of everything. Neither do we live in the passive voice, with life just happening to us. We are not doing all the doing, but neither is everything just being done to us. We live somewhere in between—in this middle, participatory voice—cooperating with God in the things that are being created through our lives. Joining this dance between *God-does* and *we-do* is essential. God speaks; we pray. God leads; we follow. God inspires; we believe. God acts; we respond. We act; God responds.

I have a friend, who I'll call John, who owns a company in a field with tremendous promise. I became aware of a huge project that a major global corporation was beginning right here in New Jersey that would necessitate massive servicing from companies in his specific area of expertise. Tens of millions of dollars in contracts would be awarded to businesses like John's. Concurrently, one of the senior executives of this global corporation was coaching me through some important decisions I was making. After ascertaining the ethical appropriateness of putting these two wonderful people in contact with one another, I was able to help John introduce his company and the services they offered to this executive, who promised to get this information to the project decision makers.

Later I asked John about his follow-up on this contact. He said something like this: "Well, I put the seed out there, and if God wants it to happen, it will just happen." I was apoplectic with concern. This means I was really ticked off. I said, maybe more vehemently than I should have, "What? You have to nurture opportunity! God wants to help you, but He can't if you just plant seeds. A farmer doesn't just go out and throw seeds on the ground. He prepares the ground, waters the seed, and fertilizes the seed. He does everything he can to provide an environment in which that seed can produce."

John Calvin in his *Institutes* wrote that "while God never slumbers or sleeps, he is inactive as if forgetting us when we are idle or mute."[3] The apostle Paul told the Corinthians that their church existed and thrived because he had planted, another leader named Apollos had watered, but God gave the increase (2 Cor. 3:6–7). He goes on to say, "For we are God's co-workers" (v. 9, TNIV).

God wants to be actively engaged in our lives, answering our prayers and helping us succeed in our arenas of possibility. But we have to cooperate!

Some of us make excuses, blaming God for our lack in so many areas of life. Do you have a business prospect? You need to prayerfully develop a business plan and then work that plan fervently. Do you have the passion and the brains to become a medical doctor? You'd better study! Do you have a marriage? You have to labor vigorously for that relationship to be everything God says it can be. You have to nurture opportunity.

It has been helpful for me to understand that God has an area of destiny for me—my unique Eden—a predestined framework for my life: "From one man he made all the nations...and he determined their boundaries" (Acts 17:26, NLT). We do not choose our destinies. But we do choose, as did Adam and Eve, whether or not to fulfill our destinies. Within that destined place we are offered choices that determine how much of what God says is possible for us will actually come to pass. We are invested in the unraveling of our own destinies.

I want to be clear about this area of destiny, or our destined place. By *place* I am not talking primarily about geography—I am talking about the predestined context of our lives. What was my life meant to be about? What is my purpose? What is my sphere of responsibility? Only in that place do I get to name possibilities. It is not possible for me, for instance, to be the president of Poland or to make decisions about the opportunities of governance there. Why? I am not Polish and that's not my place. Before I can partner with God in fulfilling my destiny, I have to discover what the boundaries of my life are. What is my destined place?

The simplest way to say this is to ask the question most of us have posed in some way many times: "What is God's will for my life?" Once I know this and pursue this, then I find that sweet spot of life—a place in which I can live and love and work and rest in confidence. In the New Testament, James strongly cautioned against arrogant presumption in the planning of our lives: "Now listen, you who say, 'Today or tomorrow we will go to this or that city, spend a year there, carry on business and make money.' Why, you do not even know what will happen tomorrow. What is your life? You are a mist that appears for a little while and then vanishes. Instead, you ought to say, 'If it is the Lord's will, we will live and do this or that'" (Jas. 4:13–15).

This and other similar passages, when misunderstood, can paralyze people and be used as an excuse for passivity or inaction. But I have come to understand that I can learn God's plan for me—I can discover my area of destiny. Then I am free, within that sphere, to "go" and make plans and "carry on business…make money…live…and do this or that." Once I discern His will for me, I am able in that place to pray, make decisions, strategize, and live boldly: "This is the confidence we have in approaching God: that if we ask anything according to his will, he hears us. And if we know that he hears us—whatever we ask—we know that we have what we asked of him" (1 John 5:14–15).

As I am writing this, I am in the early stages of my involvement on a national design team for a significant leadership initiative in New York City. Just last week, I was in a meeting with the other members of this team in a conference room at the venerable American Bible Society in uptown Manhattan. Around the table sat some leading pastors, a former mayor of a large US city, noteworthy business leaders, and representatives of several outstanding parachurch organizations. We were brainstorming around this initiative idea while fully realizing that, if successful, it has the potential to impact multiplied thousands of leaders, churches, and other institutions. Futures!

One team member, a very sincere man and owner of a large and prosperous business, spoke up to say, "Before we continue our meeting further, I think the first thing we have to decide is whether or not God wants us to do this thing." I understood exactly what he meant and thoroughly appreciated his expressed sentiment. But I was surprised by my instinctive response. This was a no-brainer for me. This idea is in line with what I believe God has called me to do. I felt "permissioned" to say yes to this possibility immediately and with confidence.

This doesn't mean that there isn't plenty for me to pray for concerning this project. Though I assume that this is something I should do, I will still carefully pray to make sure that I should continue my involvement. I will continue to pray for guidance, as I do in most every specific of my life. I will ask who, what, when, where, and how. But I begin with the premise that God brought a possibility into my area of destiny which I should name *yes*.

Chapter 7
Travel in God's Mind

W‍HAT DOES G‍OD SAY is possible for me? At the very least, I need to know this in the grand scheme in my life. Only then can I move forward by seizing all the possibilities within the parameters of His plan for me.

My meditation on 1 Corinthians 2:7–16 has helped me grasp this concept. It has helped me leave the limitations of my human thinking and travel in God's mind to discover those things that He has, from eternity, willed for this brief moment called my life.

This passage is rich with depth and is worth the effort to unpack. I will break it down into *three signal truths* that will aid us in answering the question, "What does God say is possible for me?"

> We speak of God's secret wisdom, a wisdom that has been hidden
>   and that God destined for our glory before time began....As it is
>   written:
> 'No eye has seen,
> no ear has heard,
> no mind has conceived
> what God prepared for those who love him'—
> but God has revealed it to us by his Spirit. The Spirit searches all
>   things, even the deep things of God....The man without the
>   Spirit does not accept the things that come from the Spirit of
>   God, for they are foolishness to him, and he cannot understand
>   them, because they are spiritually discerned. . . .

'For who has known the mind of the Lord

that he may instruct him?'

But we have the mind of Christ.

—1 Corinthians 2:7–16

The first truth is that before time began, God had a secret about you. This secret was His wisdom about what He had "destined for [your] glory" or "made for [your] benefit." This secret can now be known because of what Jesus did for us on the cross: He removed every impediment to the revelation and actualization of our destinies. God now wants us to know what He's planned for us: "It is the glory of God to conceal a matter; to search out a matter is the glory of kings" (Prov. 25:2).

The second truth concerns the magnitude of this secret. It's so big, so magnificent, so incredible that "no eye has seen, no ear has heard, no mind has conceived what God has prepared for those who love him" (1 Cor. 2:9). I almost always heard this passage quoted exclusively in reference to eternity and heaven's splendor. While that is fine, it's clearly not what is specifically being taught in this reading. Paul is quoting a prophecy from Isaiah 64 about how God can act in immediacy: "Oh, that you would rend the heavens and come down....For when you did awesome things that we did not expect, you came down, and the mountains trembled before you. Since ancient times no one has heard, no ear has perceived, no eye has seen any God besides you, who acts on behalf of those who wait for him" (Isa. 64:1, 3–5).

This humanly incomprehensible secret is about what God has prepared for you and me. Now. It is about our destined place and the beyond-imagination possibilities that are ours within it. The "benefits" He has planned for us are astonishing, beyond what the human eye can see, the human ear can hear, and the human mind can conceive. What God has destined for us is so expansive that it can't be comprehended with mere human ability. Whatever we see as possible for our lives from a human perspective alone, God sees much, much more.

The third truth is "God has revealed it to us by his Spirit" (1 Cor. 2:10). Whereas human eyes, ears, and minds cannot comprehend what God has planned, we can know what God wills for our lives by His Spirit: "The Spirit searches all things, even the deep things of God" (v. 10). Think about this: We can know the thoughts of God because of the Spirit of God. We can know what's in His mind concerning us and "understand what God has freely given us.... We have the mind of Christ" (vv. 12, 16). We can, by God's Spirit, travel through God's mind and know what He destined for us before the world began!

So, how? How do we travel in His mind? There are various spiritual disciplines or "means of grace" that reveal God's thoughts. These include the study of Scripture, prayer, meditation, receiving instruction from skilled teachers, learning to listen to that "still, small voice" (1 Kings 19:12, AMP). that comes from a developed awareness of God's Spirit speaking within us, opening to God's thoughts by being in committed community with other believers, and seeking the counsel of mature spiritual leaders.

There is not, however, a particular formula for coming to know God and knowing what is in His mind. This knowledge flows from our personal relationship with Him. And relationships, especially meaningful ones, are not scripted. They are unfolding adventures. Our relationship with God is uniquely exciting because we come to know our Creator. We come to know what our Designer thinks about us and has envisioned for our futures. I love these words from J. I. Packer:

> Knowing God is a relationship calculated to thrill a person's heart. What happens is that the almighty Creator...comes to you and begins to talk to you through the words and truths of Holy Scripture. Perhaps you have been acquainted with the Bible and Christian truth for many years, and it has meant little to you; but then one day you wake up to the fact that God is actually speaking to you—you!— through the biblical message.

...You come to realize as you listen that God is actually opening his heart to you, making friends with you and enlisting you as a colleague...It is a staggering thing, but it is true.[1]

I remember when one of my sons was thirteen and we were driving home after his team won a basketball game. Windows down. Sunroof open. Wind blowing through the car. Driving faster than I probably should have. U2 blaring through the stereo. I heard Bono singing:

> I want to trip inside your head
> Spend the day there.
> To hear the things you haven't said
> And see what you might see
> I want to hear you when you call
> Do you feel anything at all?
> I want to see your thoughts take shape
> And walk right out.[2]

I'm not exactly sure what Bono hoped to convey, but I thought about the promise of 1 Corinthians 2. I found myself desperate in my want to know God. Thrilled to travel in His mind. Hungry to continue searching out the secret wisdom that He wants to make known about what He's prepared for my life.

Chapter 8

See What God Sees

I CANNOT OVERSTATE HOW essential it is for our spirits to wake up to the possibilities that can only be known through a relationship with God. Scripture teaches that our spirits were dead because of our separation from God. But our spirits are made alive through faith in Jesus Christ. This is called regeneration: "We have defined regeneration to be the act of God awakening spiritual life within us, bringing us from spiritual *death* to spiritual *life*."[1]

Many people think the idea of becoming a Christian is simply for fire insurance, a foolproof way to get to heaven. Fortunately, it's so much more than that! When we come into relationship with God, we come alive to what He planned for us. We see a whole new world. We begin to see the world as He sees the world, both in its brokenness and its possibilities.

Trying to explain God things to someone whose spirit is not alive to God is like trying to explain the colors of a rainbow to a person who is blind. You can use technical or illustrative terminology to define the colors, hues, and shape of a rainbow. But it's impossible to fully grasp unless you physically see it. Discussing God stuff with someone who is spiritually asleep is often met with a blank stare. Share the same information with someone who is awake and open spiritually, and you will be met with fervent enthusiasm. This is not a criticism. It's a fact. But it's also an invitation—an invitation to join the journey, to experience this wild adventure, to move into new land. Accepting the invitation can bring our spirits alive.

In the movie *The Family Man*, Jack (played by Nicholas Cage) seems to have it all. After graduating college, he bids adieu to his sweetheart and trades a commitment to marriage for a fast-track bachelor life in New York City. He can have one of many beautiful women on most any night of the week. He has a penthouse with a view that would make Donald Trump proud. He's at the top of his world running a gargantuan corporate acquisitions firm.

But even with all of this, it becomes evident to the viewer that his life is void of higher purpose. Though he thinks he has a good life, it all changes suddenly.

Jack has an encounter with an angel and is dropped into a world that is antithetical to what he has been living. Instead of dating multiple women, he is now married to the college sweetheart he left behind, and they're raising two young, snot-nosed kids. Instead of his glorious New York City penthouse, he now lives in a middle-class neighborhood in Jersey. Instead of being a hotshot business guru, he manages his father-in-law's tire store. And, worst of all, instead of his Ferrari, he's driving a minivan.

He is initially miserable. After a bit of time, though, Jack wakes up to what life is really about. He is enlightened. He finds the joy of a committed relationship with his wife, the pleasure of caring for his children, and the simplicity of having friends who love him for who he is instead of what he has. He discovers the deep gratification of sacrificing for those he loves. He becomes aware that the condition of his soul is more important than the amount of money in his bank account. His life is now about more than pleasing himself. And he loves it.

However, the minute Jack wakes up to this better kind of life, he gets transported back to his old life in the city. He had learned the lessons he was supposed to learn. But now, though considered rich and successful, Jack is miserable. He desperately tries to get back into his Jersey-minivan-driving-tire-shop-managing world. He wants his old life—the one he never knew he had—back.

Jack wasn't necessarily a bad guy. He was like many of us. Most people don't know they are lost until they're found. Most people don't know that they're spiritually dead until they experience spiritual life.

How can we know all the possibilities that exist in the mind of God for us unless we awaken to the life God designed? How can we know the things He sees for us that human eyes can't see? Hears for us that human ears can't hear? Imagines for us that the human mind can't imagine?

So, we must discover what is in God's mind for us. Next, we must understand that within that destined-for-your-glory place, there are virtually limitless—no eye can see, no ear can hear, and no mind can conceive—possibilities. We now have choices to make as to how much of what God has prepared for us can be actualized.

I like the picture in the Old Testament of Joshua standing with the children of Israel on the borders of their promised land. After a long, tumultuous journey, they were finally able to see what God had planned for them and had promised to their father Abraham hundreds of years before their arrival. God said to Joshua, "Moses my servant is dead. Now then, you and all these people, get ready to cross the Jordan River into the land I am about to give to them—to the Israelites. I will give you every place where you set your foot, as I promised Moses. Your territory will extend from the desert to Lebanon, and from the great river, the Euphrates . . . to the Great Sea on the west" (Josh. 1:2–4).

These geographical markers delineated what God said was possible for Joshua and his followers. This was their area of destiny, the parameters of God's promise to them. It's as if God said, "How much of this do you want? What are you willing to fight for? All of this is possible for you, but you have to take it."

Once we discover what is in God's mind for us, we have to make choices. How much of what God says is possible do we want to realize? What are we willing to pray for, work for, risk for, and sacrifice for? God loves us just the same, regardless of how much of what He has promised us we actually pursue. As much as I revel in being loved, however, I was made for even more than knowing I am loved. I want to partner with God to see His mission in this world successfully achieved.

Carla Ceasar was nominated for her second Emmy Award for a public service announcement her young production company produced about the refugee crisis in Darfur. She mentioned this to me in her characteristically unassuming way, as I sat with her and her husband, Raleigh, in a café in South Orange, New Jersey, owned by a mutual friend of ours. We were listening to a jazz band play and watching the young phenom, Maurice Chestnut, of Broadway's *Bring In Da Noise, Bring In Da Funk* fame, do a marvelous tap dance interpretation of the music. Especially impressive was Maurice's duet with a percussionist, Manolo Badrena, formerly of Spyro Gyra. It was a fun night!

Over the sound of the music, Carla began to tell me how her mind had opened to new possibilities when she became a Christ follower. She began praying most every day—in response to the principles being shared in this book—about possibilities. "Lord, how do you want to use me to create preferred futures?" My heart started beating fast when she said that! The music was great, but her story was even better.

Carla said that although she had experienced success as a freelance producer, including an Emmy nomination for some of her work at

WWOR-TV, she began to believe that God had put it in her heart to start her own company…and so she did. Soon thereafter, she was discussing the movie *Hotel Rwanda* and the Darfur crisis with a production assistant. The PA proposed creating a public service announcement using Don Cheadle, the star of *Hotel Rwanda* for which he received an Academy Award nomination, and Paul Rusesabagina, the hero portrayed by Cheadle in the movie. The PA thought they could rally some Hollywood executives to fund a project like this. Carla admits that her first response was not positive: "This is crazy. Our company is too young. This idea is too expensive. A big star won't want to donate his time for this. How would we get Mr. Rusesabagina here from Rwanda? It's impossible!"

But then she said that she chose to see this potential project through God's eyes. Was this idea an answer to the prayers she had been praying? Could she act to create a preferred future for the countless people who would be helped by this undertaking? She began to believe that God brought her this concept—that it was in line with what she was meant to do.

So she named this idea…*possible.*

Within a few weeks, Cheadle, Rusesabagina, several major New York executives, and a production studio were partnered with Carla, all donating their time, services, and expenses to produce this widely recognized and highly awarded piece, which was clearly created to serve a higher good. Carla made a decision within her area of destiny to think bigger. To choose more rather than less. To believe. To act. To risk. And to ultimately actualize something that she believed was within the parameters of God's plan for her life.

Chapter 9

God's Self-Limitation

God...could do anything, anywhere, at any time, by any means. But he doesn't. He confines Himself to the redemptive processes worked through the Cross of His Son and released by the ministry of the Holy Spirit through the Church His Son redeemed. He will do nothing outside those channels. That is not to say there is nothing else He could do; it is to say, though, that there is no other way He will.

—Jack Hayford,
Prayer Is Invading the Impossible[1]

DO WE DECIDE WHAT is possible for God?

Of this I am sure: we decide, to some degree, what is possible for God to do through us. In His sovereignty, God has decided, to a great extent, to limit His involvement in this world to the willingness of human beings.

Dorothy Sayers wrote about the three humiliations of God: the incarnation (God becoming a man through Jesus Christ), the cross, and the church.[2] It is amazing that God has so reduced Himself in order to win the willful participation of people in their relationships with Him and the fulfilling of His purposes and their destinies. He absolutely insists that we deliberately cooperate with Him in order to complete the human story. What a responsibility—what an opportunity. We are privileged to join with God in actualizing His plans for our futures and the future: "All this is from God, who reconciled us to himself through Christ and gave us the ministry of reconciliation....And he has committed to us the message of reconciliation. We are therefore Christ's ambassadors" (2 Cor. 5:18–20).

How do we cooperate with God? Prayer is one of the most important ways. Prayer is how we communicate to God, revealing our willingness to participate with Him. Prayer is essential to that delicate dance of He-does/we-do because it is our invitation to God to show up and empower us to do His work. Prayer also guides us as we choose possibilities. James wrote that "[we] have not, because [we] ask not" (Jas. 4:2, KJV). The Bible tells us that there are many things that are potentially ours that will not be realized unless we ask God for them.

I'm struck by how often God says things like, "Seek Me and find Me" (Jer. 29:13, NKJV). A legitimate question is, If He wants so badly to be found, why should we have to seek Him? The answer takes us back to His first choice concerning human beings. Think about it this way: He willed that we would will for His will to be done in our lives. We need to understand that God is often saying, "I have wonderful things for you, but you have to 'Ask to receive, seek to find, and knock in order for doors to be open.'" (See Matthew 7:7.) John Wesley said, "God will do nothing on earth except in answer to believing prayer."[3]

How many possibilities are not realized in my life because I simply don't ask and then follow through on the asking by cooperating with God in seeing these things fully realized?

It is said that when the early leaders of New York City prepared some version of a master plan in order to anticipate its future growth, they only envisioned the city expanding to 19th Street. They then named 19th Street Boundary, or Bound, Street. It is still called Bound Street today. The city, though, has flourished all the way—at last count—to 285th Street.

We must not be limited by 19th-Street thinking. We must not limit God with our limited thinking. He is "able to do immeasurably more than all we ask or imagine, according to his power that is at work within us" (Eph. 3:20). So, dream big! Pray big! Decide big! Plan big! And act big!

There are countless possibilities awaiting you in your place of destiny. But you have to name them *possible* in order to bring them to pass.

I have a mentoring relationship with a lawyer. Several times we have been in meetings where big ideas—blue-sky ideas—were discussed. I noticed that his initial response was to conjure consternation on his face and then proceed to "lawyer" the idea to near death. You know what I mean by "lawyer": lawyers are often paid to consider all the things that could go wrong and to attempt to mitigate risk as much as is practical. We have all heard the commercials for some supposed wonder drug where the announcer spends more time warning you of terrible side effects than actually marketing the benefits of the drug. Thank the lawyers.

Well, my lawyer friend is an outstanding person with high-caliber leadership capacity. I recently brought up this proclivity to immediately focus on the negative. "Are you aware that your first response to a big idea is to discuss what could go wrong?" I asked. "That though you always come around to the positive, your first instinct is contrarian?"

He was surprised. But as he mentally replayed our meetings, he said quickly, "You know, you're right. I've been trained to see what could go wrong. I need to be retrained to see what could go right."

It was the baseball season. We're both dads who've watched our kids play many games. The first instinct of young outfielders is to run forward when the ball is hit their way because it looks like the ball is going to drop in front of them. More often than not, much to the outfielders' embarrassment, the ball flies over their heads. Bad things happen when a ball goes over an outfielder's head. Coaches repeatedly attempt to retrain this instinct to run forward when the ball comes off the bat. They tell their players over and over, "When a ball is hit in the air toward you, your first step must always be back." That may sound simple, but kids have a very difficult time redeveloping that first-step instinct.

I said to my friend, "You have to retrain your first-step instinct toward what could go right. You must develop a possibility instinct. You must see the potential of a preferred future. Your first thought should be, 'What if?' After that, perform your due diligence. Do commission feasibility studies. Do a risk analysis. Review contracts, and do all of that important lawyer stuff. But start with a focus on what's possible."

What do our faces say when we face possibility? Our faces usually communicate what is going on in the deepest part of our being: "Interestingly, 'growing up' is largely a matter of learning to hide our spirit behind our face, eyes, and language so that we can evade and manage others to achieve what we want and avoid what we fear. By contrast, the child's face is a constant epiphany because it doesn't yet know how to do this. It cannot manage its face."[4]

My lawyer friend's face immediately conveyed his instinct to doubt when presented with an outside-of-the-usual idea. Oscar Wilde wrote that we have the face we deserve by the time we are forty. That's a little frightening. We speak about saving face; I also think we can change our face from "what?" to "what if?"

The story is told that President Thomas Jefferson was once traveling across country on horseback with a group of trusted companions. They came to a river that was swollen because of a recent downpour. The bridge at the crossing had been washed away, and each rider was forced to attempt to cross the river on horseback. The currents were rapid. The danger of drowning threatened each rider. There was a stranger standing by who needed to cross the river. He watched as several riders plunged into the water at great risk but made it to the other side. This stranger asked President Jefferson if he could ride double and be carried to the other side.

The president immediately agreed. At double the risk, he took his horse skillfully through the raging water and safely to the opposite bank.

As the stranger dismounted and settled back on dry ground, someone in the group challenged him as to why he had asked the president of the United States to take him across the river under these circumstances. The stranger was stunned and admitted that he had no idea that it was the president who had aided him. "'All I know,' he said, 'is that on some of your faces was written the answer 'no,' and on some of them was the answer 'yes.' His was a 'yes face.'"[5]

When God brings me the possibilities He has prepared for me within my area of destiny, what does my face say? When I see feasibilities that are beyond human imagination, what is my instinctive response? I can choose to call those God-made opportunities anything I will, so I want everything in my inner being to be reflected through an unqualified "yes!" face. I choose to name these things...*possible*.

Part Two

Reflection Questions

1. What possibilities may God have shown you to which you have said, "No," "Maybe," or "Someday"—or perhaps that you have named impossible? Why? Write each present possibility down and name it "possible."

2. Review 1 Corinthians 2:7–10. How does this passage help you discover your potential areas of destiny?

3. What are some spiritual practices that will help you travel in God's mind to discover what God says is possible for you?

4. Do you see how becoming aware of what God says is possible for you can liberate Him to do the "more and better" things he has planned for your life?

Part Three

IMAGINE

Chapter 10
Positive Audaciousness

au·da·cious (P) Pronunciation Key (ȯ -'dā-shəs) adj.

Invulnerable to fear or intimidation	Reckless
Fearlessly bold	Rash
Spirited and original	Unrestrained by propriety
Positive	Negative

ON JUNE 12, 1987, President Ronald Reagan stood behind a podium in front of the Berlin Wall and made a strong, yet almost desperate appeal to a Communist dictator. One line sums up the eloquent, thirty-minute speech:

"Mr. Gorbachev, tear down this wall."

At that time in history, a policy given the apt acronym MAD—mutually assured destruction—dismally positioned the world at a standstill. This policy dictated that if the Soviet Union launched a nuclear attack against America, we would retaliate in the same way. Both countries would destroy each other. While this policy was developed as a preventative measure to discourage a full-scale nuclear war, it challenged logic and left millions of people wondering who would strike first and when. The future looked bleak. Many thought this was the beginning of the end of the world, and MAD seemed to be the best strategy anyone could imagine.

In the early 1980s, when West Berlin was hauntingly surrounded by the infamous wall, I was privileged to speak at a local church that was established to care for United States soldiers serving there. West Berlin was dominated by the military presence of the Four Powers. The palpable global tensions were impossible to ignore. I spent time listening to the soldiers' stories. These young men and women were faced with the stark reality of being stationed on the frontlines of the Cold War. This surreal setting influenced their thoughts about God, enticing them to think about their futures and the future of the world.

Peter Robinson, the speechwriter who penned the words "tear down this wall," wrote a book about his experience working for President Reagan. He chronicled the story around Reagan's speech—his bold and controversial challenge to the Soviet Union. Robinson divulged background information about the broader context that caused Reagan to communicate his dream of a better, free world.

Years before Reagan was elected president, the speechwriter narrates, he believed "we [would] win and they [would] lose."[1] This bold assertion was viewed by many people—including some of his close political advisors—as naïveté, as simplistic thinking, and as dangerous idealism. "He'd had to be able to envision a United States willing to marshal its military, economical, and technological superiority as never before, subjecting the Soviet Union to pressures that were new, intense, and sustained."[2]

Reagan believed that the wall would come down, that communism would be annihilated, and that all human beings would live in a better world. One particular sentence Robinson wrote has stuck in my mind: "Simple as it was... the President's strategy had required him to engage in an *audacious act of imagination*."[3] Reagan was convinced a greater future could exist. By conceiving this preferred future through his audacious act of imagination and by motivating the free world to get behind his vision, Reagan changed the course of history. The world embarked on a new era.

All...have goals. But there is a difference between merely having a goal and becoming committed to a huge, daunting challenge—like a big mountain to climb.

—James Collins & Jerry Porras,
Built to Last[4]

Built to Last, written by James Collins and Jerry Porras, discusses visionary companies. According to their research, visionary companies do not profit solely financially. They impact the world in significant and positive ways over a long period of time. One of the eight identifiable characteristics of such "built to last" companies was this: all of them had a "BHAG"—a Big Hairy Audacious Goal.[5] Every great company has a goal that's audacious—intrepidly daring and fearlessly bold—a dauntless ambition that most companies would never have the guts to believe for.

Great leaders have BHAGs. Reagan's BHAG was the destruction of communism and the creation of a freer global society. John F. Kennedy declared his when he told the world the United States was going to be the first country to send a man to the moon. Today, this mission seems quite pedestrian. In 1961, it was thought premature, even presumptuous.

When Martin Luther King stood on the National Mall on August 28, 1963, and told the world his dream, he verbalized it in a way unknown throughout modern history:

> I have a dream that one day...this nation will rise up and live out the true meaning of its creed...the heat of injustice will be transformed into an oasis of freedom...my four little children will one day...not be judged by the color of their skin but by the content of their character...I have a dream today!

King saw beyond the reality of racial injustice at that time—where African Americans had to drink from separate water fountains, sit in the back of public buses, and, in some places, were still not even allowed to vote. Through an audacious act of imagination, King was able to "see" his dream as a physical reality before it was accomplished. Though much work still needs to be done on this front, there is no question that much progress has been made. I continually see this dream realized when I preach at our church weekend after weekend and look out at the nearly fifty nationalities and ethnicities that make up our one congregation.

Now faith is being sure of what we hope for and certain of what we do not see.

—Hebrews 11:1

Those dreamers and leaders changed the world. What about us? What can we do?

If we want to create a preferred future for ourselves and for others, we must have an audacious imagination; we must see the future before it can be seen. We must partner with God who has such an imagination that we cannot even begin to comprehend its magnitude and power! God is described as He who "calls things that are not as though they were" (Rom. 4:17) and "creates new things out of nothing" (NLT).

We must also learn to articulate to ourselves and to those we are leading what we imagine, constantly keeping our imaginings in focus in order for us to purpose our lives around bringing them to pass.

In the Old Testament, the Israelites had a creative way of remembering the statutes and precepts given to them by God. They would write selected verses of the Law on tiny strips of parchment, wrap them in tiny cases called frontlets, or phylacteries, and literally wear them on their foreheads. They were symbolically designed to connect their thoughts with God's words. While the idea seems kind of radical, the point is clear: it would be impossible to forget God's vision for their lives because it was right between their eyes. Similarly, our dreams, our visions, our BHAGs need to be like frontlets before our own eyes. We must constantly call them to mind.

Our futures depend on it. The futures of those we are leading depend on it.

The inner world of meditation is most easily entered through the door of the imagination. We fail today to appreciate its tremendous power. The imagination is stronger than conceptual thought and stronger than the will.

—Richard Foster,
The Celebration of Discipline[6]

Richard Foster wrote his classic *Celebration of Discipline* about the spiritual habits that God uses to engage actively in our lives. Among disciplines such as prayer, fasting, and corporate worship, Foster explores meditation. The principal portal of meditation, he suggests, is the imagination.

I want to propose a new discipline: the "discipline of imagining." We must intentionalize imagining—deliberately and prayerfully imaging the specific things we believe God has said are possible for us. We must regularly practice this in the same manner as we engage in other spiritual practices. "We simply must become convinced of the importance of thinking and experiencing in images."[7]

As children, tapping into our imaginations was spontaneous, an innate gift that could be activated without much thought or effort. With faithful ease, little kids can imagine almost anything, including playmates. I can remember my own imaginary worlds when I was a young boy. In my mind, I was the star of a full-blown basketball game played on the hardwood floor of my bedroom, or a lawyer arguing a case in front of a jury, or, of all things, a preacher using great oratorical skills to move a large crowd.

"Just as children need to learn to think logically, adults need to rediscover the magical reality of the imagination."[8] As adults, many of us have been conditioned to disregard the imagination, even to such a degree that we fear it. We need, however, to become reacquainted with the imagination, using the art of imaging to invigorate and fortify the realities God has called us to create.

Imaging, the forming of mental pictures or images, is based on the principle that there is a deep tendency in human nature to ultimately become precisely like that which we imagine or image ourselves as being.... In imaging, one does not merely think about a hoped-for goal; one "sees" or visualizes it with tremendous intensity, reinforced by prayer.

—Norman Vincent Peale,
Positive Imaging[9]

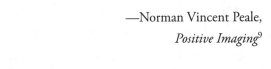

We must spend time feeding our imagination and visualizing preferred futures. We must see preferred reality with the eyes of our hearts before it can be seen with our physical eyes. As believers, all this imagining must be done, of course, within our areas of destiny. We've learned about the necessity of traveling in God's mind, of seeing what God sees for us, and of discovering the boundaries of what God says is possible for our lives. Within that place we can make choices that determine how much of that possibility can actually happen. Accordingly, our imagination cannot operate positively outside of the parameters of God's plans. When we imagine outside of that context, audacious imagining can become a negative practice.

Audaciousness can be:

- positive or negative
- bold or overconfident
- brave or brazen
- fearless or shameless
- lion-hearted or harebrained
- valorous or heedless
- adventuresome or reckless

We must exercise positive audaciousness within the framework of what God has destined our lives to be about. We must imagine things that exist in His mind, things that are better, best, and preferred.

This is not about visualizing a bigger house, a more luxurious car, or a more expensive watch. While these things are not inherently wrong, I want to inspire ideas that are greater than self-centered materialism. We ought not to waste our imaginations on things that do not promote a higher moral value. Our imagination is to be used God's way—for His purpose and plan for us. Only when we use God's channel can He "do immeasurably more than all we ask or imagine, according to his power that is at work within us" (Eph. 3:20).

Unfortunately, out of sincere misgivings, we often fear becoming negatively audacious and refuse to believe for anything grand. Our imaginations then lie dormant and are essentially useless. Rather than limiting ourselves by being afraid of negative audaciousness, we need to practice positive audaciousness. Positive audaciousness is imagining audaciously in line with God's plan for our lives.

Chapter 11
Creative Audaciousness

HUMAN AUDACIOUSNESS BASED ON God's audaciousness is the ultimate creative audaciousness.

Genesis 30 records one of my favorite Bible stories, which serves as an ingenious example of creative audaciousness. Abraham had a son named Isaac who bore a son named Jacob. God made incredible promises to those three men. He vowed to bless them and their families so that through them a nation would be birthed that would bless the entire world.

When Jacob was a young man, he got himself into trouble at home and consequently fled to a distant land. There he came into a business relationship with Laban, the patriarch of a large family. What Jacob didn't know was that Laban—who would later become his father-in-law—also happened to be a less-than-honest businessman. Jacob was hired as the manager of Laban's business, raising and breeding livestock such as sheep, goats, and cattle. Being blessed with a sharp mind and, more importantly, by God Himself, Jacob worked hard. The herds and flocks grew. Business exponentially prospered under his skillful management.

Laban, infamous for dishonestly arranging Jacob's marriage to the wrong daughter, also unfairly swindled Jacob out of a percentage of the considerable company profits that rightfully belonged to him. This young man, unfortunately, didn't read the fine print or get the right attorney when he signed his employment contract. While there was a direct relationship between the business's astronomic success and Jacob's savvy business sense, Laban refused to share the profits with him. Burdened by frustration, Jacob eventually mustered the courage to question his boss: "Hey Laban, I'm a great manager. I've made you rich and successful. Now, what about me? I'd like to share in some of these profits!" I have a feeling Laban rolled his eyes and shrugged his shoulders in irritation as he replied, "Well, what do you want?"

Jacob answered him, "Don't give me anything at all. Just do this one thing, and I'll go back to work for you. Let me go out among your flocks today and remove all the sheep and goats that are speckled or spotted, along with all the dark-colored sheep. Give them to me as my wages. This will make it easy for you to see whether or not I have been honest. If you find in my flock any white sheep or goats that are not speckled, you will know that I have stolen them from you" (Gen. 30:31–33, NLT).

Speckled, spotted, and dark-colored sheep and goats were the rarest of animals, but this is exactly how Jacob wanted to get paid. Laban granted his request and the deal was sealed. When Jacob went to bed that night, Laban went about his underhanded, crafty ways. He gathered all the animals that were speckled, spotted, and dark in color and stashed them a three-day trip away from Jacob's camp.

All was not lost for Jacob, for he had an unusual yet God-inspired plan to grow his part of the business. What he did next was quite odd:

> Now Jacob took fresh shoots from poplar, almond, and plane trees and peeled off strips of the bark to make white streaks on them. Then he set up these peeled branches beside the watering troughs so Laban's flocks would see them as they came to drink, for that was when they mated. So when the flocks mated in front of the white-streaked branches, all of their offspring were streaked, speckled, and spotted. Jacob added them to his own flock, thus separating the lambs from Laban's flock. Then at mating time, he turned the flocks toward the streaked and dark-colored rams in Laban's flock. This

is how he built his flock from Laban's....As a result, Jacob's flocks increased rapidly, and he became very wealthy, with many servants, camels, and donkeys.

—Genesis 30:37–43, NLT

How on earth did this happen? Commentator Matthew Henry wrote that it was by "the power of Jacob's imagination"[1] that God showed up and worked miracles. Jacob articulated into those branches what he pictured for his future; he saw what could be before it actually was.

Two really important things occur here: *First, Jacob's imaginings were based on what he believed God had promised him. Second, God responded to what Jacob believed.*

Jacob didn't make up this idea on his own. He got it from God. I read this story for years before I fully understood this. When Jacob explains his success to Rachel and Leah, we discover that it was God who had put this bizarre vision into his heart:

"During the mating season, I had a dream....The angel of God said to me, 'Jacob!' And I replied, 'Yes, I'm listening!' The angel said, 'Look, and you will see that only the streaked, speckled, and spotted males are mating with the females of your flock. For I have seen all that Laban has done to you. I am the God you met at Bethel, the place where you anointed the pillar of stone and made a vow to serve me.'"

—Genesis 31:10–13, NLT

Jacob's imagination was based on this specific idea he received from God and was also motivated by prophesied blessings God gave him earlier in his life at a place called Bethel. While on the run from his past, Jacob had spent a night at Bethel and had a dream that changed his life forever. God spoke to him:

"I am the Lord, the God of your grandfather Abraham and the God
of your father, Isaac. The ground you are lying on belongs to you. I
will give it to you and your descendants. Your descendants will be as
numerous as the dust of the earth! They will cover the land from east
to west and from north to south. All the families of the earth will
be blessed through you and your descendants. What's more, I will
be with you, and I will protect you wherever you go. I will someday
bring you safely back to this land. I will be with you constantly until
I have finished giving you everything I have promised."

—Genesis 28:13–15, NLT

Many years after that paramount promise, Jacob realized his preferred
future had not come to pass. He was shocked that he had not yet been
blessed according to God's promises. At this pivotal moment in his life,
Jacob was reminded that his life was, in fact, destined for more. His imagination was profoundly informed by the blessing he knew was in God's
mind for him.

Jacob's audaciousness was based on God's audaciousness.

Have we become content with less rather than more? Dissatisfaction
needs to stir us if we look at our lives and see anything other than what
we know God has imagined for us. You probably have had your own
version of a Bethel experience. Maybe you had specific ideas—speckled,
spotted, and rare ideas—new realities to create that seemed almost crazy.
If you believe God gave you those thoughts, you must not dare imagine
anything less.

Perhaps you felt called to financial independence and the freedom to do
good that it brings, but instead you find yourself captive to debt. Perhaps
you dreamed about owning your own "higher purpose" business, but
instead you feel like you are owned by someone else's "lower purpose" business. Perhaps you envisioned finding an outlet for your creative and artistic
talents, but instead you know only empty survival. You must insist on

realizing your promised blessings in your destined place. Imagine that great God thing, act accordingly, and watch Him show up and work miracles to bring it to pass. God has an audacious imagination about your future!

Chapter 12

Prophetic Audaciousness

FAITH AND IMAGINATION ARE interconnected.

Faith brings power—the power of believing something that we hold in our minds to be true.

By faith, we see something that doesn't yet physically exist. Most every living thing responds to faith, especially articulated faith. Jacob articulated what he believed by carving his vision into branches. Each and every one of us needs to imagine, believe, and carve our own branches in our own ways. You can write your imagination into a mission statement for your family or your business. You can design your vision into a blueprint for a new building. You can detail positive expectations for your children by regularly speaking to them about God's unique destiny for their lives.

Imaginings become prophetic when articulated. These types of "prophecies" have been researched extensively within the field of psychology. Experts have generally accepted the theory that what human beings believe and communicate has a powerful influence over what happens in their lives.

Self-imposed prophesy is where our lives respond to what we believe about ourselves. Studies have shown that people speak out loud at a rate of about 150 to 200 words per minute, but internally we talk to ourselves at a rate of about 1,300 words per minute. We are all in rapid monologue, perpetually self-prophesying. Think about this for a minute. What do you believe about yourself? What do you say to yourself?

Our emotions are activated by what we believe. Dr. William Backus, psychologist and author of twenty books on counseling and pastoral-related matters, defines emotions like this: "a response of a number of physical systems to something we believe."[1] We interpret situations based on our belief systems. I've heard many people say, for instance, that fear is faith moving in the wrong direction. We are afraid because we have faith that something bad is going to happen.

Say I walk into our kitchen in the dark hours of the morning. I see a person standing in the shadows of the room. If I believe that person is a burglar, my emotions—as experienced through my physical systems—are going to respond accordingly. I would be terribly excited. My heart would beat faster. My blood pressure would rise. I would prepare to protect my family. I hope I wouldn't run! However, if I believe the person in the shadows is my daughter unexpectedly home, I would be joyfully excited—though my heart would still beat faster and my blood pressure would still rise—and I would rush to give her a big hug!

Even our physiology, therefore, is affected by what we say to ourselves.

What the BLEEP Do We Know!? is a movie about quantum physics and the relationship between God and science. There is a vignette about an experiment conducted by a Japanese scientist. He wanted to determine if and how droplets of water responded to positive and negative energies in the form of words. Water droplets were put into two separate jars. To one jar, positive words such as "love" and "thank you" were communicated. Negative phrases, including "you make me sick" and "I will kill you," were conveyed to the other jar.

There was a significant difference between the responses of the different sets of water droplets. Somehow, the water in the "positive" jar transformed into beautiful shapes and the appearance of the negative ones turned ugly.

"Makes you wonder, doesn't it?" voiced the narrator. "If thoughts can do that to water, imagine what our thoughts can do to us."

Entire communities are also influenced by what they believe and say about themselves. About seventeen years ago, West Orange, NJ, was a community in rapid decline. The mayor—who had served well for many years—sadly encountered a sudden outbreak of corruption in his administration. For a variety of reasons, the township began to appear to deteriorate. Property values were declining, a titanic amount of negative publicity tarnished the town's image, and people complained vociferously about community taxes, crime rates, and the educational system.

The town council decided to create a public relations committee, led by the CEO of what was the largest advertising firm in New Jersey. I was appointed to be a part of this strategic commission. Our charge was to study the cause of the real and perceived negative issues confronting our town, to explore what was right about West Orange, and to craft an effective strategy to reinvent our public image. Over the course of the next few months, we held meetings with every elected official, the chief of police, the superintendent of schools, and other key community stakeholders. After much research, we determined that perhaps the main reason for our town's plight was its self-perception.

While West Orange had suffered some very real setbacks, there really was much to be enthusiastic about in our community. The residents, however, glumly went about their daily business thinking and verbalizing negative feelings about the town going "down," and thus the town underwent its own version of self-imposed prophecy. West Orange was, in fact, going down! After reporting back to the town council, we were empowered to set up a public relations infrastructure with the initial task of marketing West Orange to West Orange. We introduced the WOW campaign—West Orange Wonderful—and motivated the residents to start talking about all of the reasons we love our community.

In due season, my good friend John McKeon, then the council president, was elected mayor. He brought a renewed positive energy and agenda to our town. Since that time, property values have soared. Many people who thought about leaving have stayed. A reinvestment was made into our school system, and the *Washington Post* now ranks it in the top 1 percent in the nation. I genuinely believe the turnaround in West Orange had much to do with how the community changed the way it thought and spoke about itself.

Sometimes we have to market faith and hope about ourselves to ourselves. What we believe and say about ourselves powerfully affects life reality. Moreover, what other people believe and say about us and what we believe and say about other people is just as influential. *This is called others-imposed prophesy—how the expectations of one person governs another's actions.*[2]

People around us respond to what we imagine and communicate about them to them. I recently saw a high school basketball coach attempt to motivate a group of talented athletes by telling them how terrible they were. What utter foolishness! The team conformed to what their leader believed about them. Likewise, a negative parent can make it very difficult for a teenager to develop into a positive adult. And a nagging spouse will usually get what they confess.

Expectations do influence behavior. I challenge you to love people enough to see the best in them and their future, even if that means using your imagination. Make the discipline of positive imagining intentional, and prophesy audaciously over those you love, sometimes in spite of what you see. Then watch as what you imagine comes to pass!

In a fascinating study exploring the Pygmalion effect,[3] a group of elementary school teachers were told that 20 percent of their students showed unusual potential for intellectual growth. The names of these "special" students were drawn randomly in this blind study; they did not technically have the potential that was suggested. Eight months later, however, these children showed significant gains in IQ when compared to the students who were not singled out. These children radically improved not because they were smarter than their peers, but because their teachers simply believed in them and unknowingly communicated their faith.

What does this have to do with audacious imaginations? With prophetic audaciousness? The image we hold, even for others, of a preferred future ultimately informs their thinking, their lives, and their realities!

Without a doubt, self- and others-imposed prophecies are powerful practices, but neither of them is nearly as effectual as what I like to call God-imposed prophecy. A God-imposed prophecy has to do with what God imagines in His mind and speaks into a person's heart about the preferred future He sees. This is what Jacob responded to when he carved those branches.

It's a widely known fact that when one visits Israel, there is a tremendous disparity between the appearance of the land owned and stewarded by the Jews and that of the Muslims. I realize this is a complicated and controversial subject and that there are enormous political and systemic issues that contribute to this. I believe, however, that the real key has to do with what God imagined for the Jews thousands of years ago: "The desert and the parched land will be glad; the wilderness will rejoice and blossom. Like the crocus, it will burst into bloom.... Water will gush forth in the wilderness and streams in the desert. The burning sand will become a pool, and the thirsty ground bubbling springs" (Isa. 35:1–2, 6–7).

When Darrow Miller was a student in Israel, he went on a school trip and visited a desert there. He was fascinated when he saw a small forest that grew on a hill in the middle of this barren wasteland. When Miller questioned his professor about this anomaly, he learned that this forest was purposely planted by the Israelis: "There were two different visions for this land. The Israelis...believed God when he said this was a land flowing with milk and honey. The Palestinians believe Allah has cursed the land."[4] The land was the same, but because the visions were different, so were the results. The Israelis expected a garden to grow in the desert not because they were experts in botany or agriculture, but because they responded to God's expectations for them.

If we feel like we are living in a barren place but know that God has prophesied fertility there, we need to get busy expecting God's reality. We must use audacious imaginings to plant seed, irrigate, and cultivate gardens in the desert to ensure that our future lines up with what we know God has planned for our lives. Audacious? You bet! But if our audaciousness is based on God's audaciousness, we can then create better, best, and preferred futures. The combination of His promises and our faith guarantees gushing waters and blooming flowers…regardless of the present appearance of infertile ground.

Chapter 13
Refined Audaciousness

AUDACIOUS FAITH IS NOT a simplistic belief that is untested or unrefined by the realities of life. Life isn't easy. Many of us have suffered disappointments that have hindered or maybe nearly obliterated our faith. Every day I'm reminded of the kinds of things that can happen in life that cause our faith, especially audacious imaginings, to be challenged.

I'm thinking about my friends Heidi and Phil. As college students, this young couple led a campus ministry at MIT. After graduating college, they committed their lives to serving the people in Israel. Their journey has been slow, hard, and long. Their ministry hasn't always been well received. And, in an unspeakable tragedy, their fourteen-year-old daughter, Abigail, was killed by a suicide bomber.

This was much on my mind when I spoke about the power of an audacious imagination at a leadership conference they sponsored in Israel earlier this year. How can someone who has suffered what they suffer still nurture audacious imaginings for a better future? Yet Phil and Heidi do. They still dream for a greater future for their adopted homeland. They still envision great things for their four surviving children. They are still willing to sacrifice their lives for what they believed prior to their daughter's senseless murder. This isn't a naïve faith. It's a faith that chooses to stand back up after inconceivable tragedy and still believe.

Scripture tells us that we "rejoice in our sufferings, because we know that suffering produces perseverance; perseverance, character; and character, hope" (Rom. 5:3–4). Somehow, the setbacks, disappointments, and loss we experience must morph into an even greater hope. This is not immature faith but is, as M. Scott Peck wrote, a "mature faith, the kind of faith which comes after we've asked the hard questions." Oliver Wendell Holmes, former US Supreme Court justice, once said, "I don't give a fig for the simplicity this side of complexity, but I would die for the simplicity on the other side."[1] Simple faith is faith that has been refined through the complexities of life.

We all experience life setbacks. We all have the opportunity to choose how we will allow these misfortunes to influence our faith and our futures. Will difficulties and disappointments crush us? Or will we turn our adversities into something more powerful than themselves, something that can beneficially impact our lives and the lives of others?

Daniel Defoe's *Robinson Crusoe* is one of the most popular adventure novels in history. A young Crusoe set off on a voyage out to sea in search of a life of adventure. After enduring a shipwreck in which he was the sole survivor, he suffered a chain of misfortunes. Crusoe found himself cast away on a remote island. He was repeatedly chased by wild animals and hounded by belligerent natives. He endured severe bouts of loneliness and depression. During a particularly painful time, he started to panic at his devastating predicament. He then decided to write a two-column list juxtaposing the "Good" versus "Evil" aspects of his ordeal.

Under the Evil column, he wrote, "I am cast upon a horrible desolate island, void of all hope of recovery." This was countered with a Good statement: "But I am alive, and not drowned, as all my ship's company was." Crusoe continued, "I have no soul to speak to, or relieve me…but God wonderfully sent the ship in near enough to the shore, that I have gotten out so many necessary things as will either supply my wants, or enable me to supply myself even as long as I live." And the list goes on.

Crusoe closed his compare-and-contrast experiment with these words: "Upon the whole, here was an undoubted testimony that there was scarce any condition in the world so miserable but there was something negative or something positive to be thankful for in it."[2] In spite of his circumstances, he made a conscious decision to keep believing the best for his future. Even in his barren place, Crusoe cultivated a better life for himself up until the time he was rescued.

Setbacks must not destroy our audaciousness. They must be leveraged toward future victories! In the 1960s, Scott Paper dominated the paper-based marketplace but was instantaneously booted into second place when Proctor & Gamble stormed their proverbial castle and took over the number-one spot. Scott Paper apparently stuck their tail between their legs and accepted their new, lower rank. The ambience of this company was generally depressing, and any flicker of morale was quickly stamped out. The leaders seemed to give up without a fight.

However, another competitor in this industry, Kimberly-Clark, saw an opportunity to battle the giant and win. They were convinced that the presence of fierce competition would help motivate them to create new ideas, products, and strategies that would give them an edge over Proctor & Gamble. They imagined becoming number one. In one of the most memorable meetings in the company's history, the CEO of Kimberly-Clark stood up and announced a moment of silence. When the silence was over, he declared, "That was a moment of silence for P&G!" Everyone went wild! It was no coincidence that Kimberly-Clark moved into their future with an unwavering faith and ultimately secured the top position in the paper business. This is called "unwavering faith amid the brutal facts."[3]

I like that idea. We need to stand in the midst of our battles and have a moment of silence for our enemies. Have a moment of silence for the obstacles that try to defeat us. Have a moment of silence for the fear that tries to dominate our spirits. Have a moment of silence for the sickness that tries to take us out. In the Psalms, David writes, "Though an army besiege me, my heart will not fear; though war break out against me, even then will I be confident.... Then my head will be exalted above the enemies who surround me; at his tabernacle I will sacrifice with shouts of joy; I will sing and make music to the LORD" (Ps. 27:3, 6).

Great leaders endure great challenges, but the outcome is always the same. Each one of them transcends their oppressive circumstances with a deeper and more refined faith. During a devastating, yet particularly pivotal season in his life, Norman Vincent Peale, author of the landmark book *The Power of Positive Thinking*, found himself venting to his wife on a London park bench. He voiced a litany of the discouragement, negativity, and hopelessness he was feeling.

His wife challenged him in response to his depressing monologue. She told him he needed a conversion, a deep encounter with God. "You are not only my husband, but my pastor," she told him. "In the latter department...I am increasingly disappointed in you. I hear you from the pulpit talking about faith and trust in God's wondrous power. But now I hear in you no faith or trust at all...You need to be converted."[4] Peale then began to pray. He confessed his weaknesses and had an encounter with God that could be described as nothing less than supernatural. This was a defining moment in his life.

Peale also wrote about his natural tendencies for stress and tension. Picture that! This positive thinking pioneer did not wake up one day with an unwavering, optimistic attitude and life outlook. No! He developed it through wrestling with a propensity for stress and tension. The positive attitude he spent his lifetime promoting was birthed through suffering in a deep place in his soul.

When I entered the ministry some thirty years ago, I was young and full of faith, much of it, I'm sure, naïve. Over the years, I have experienced the ebb and flow of life. Like most leaders, I've had my share of heartbreak. I've made some stupid decisions. I've been rejected by supposed friends. I've had tremendous setbacks. Frankly, at times I've wondered whether or not I'd make it to the future I knew God had planned for me. But here I am, by God's grace, all these years later. And I'm more excited and realistically idealistic than ever! I love God more deeply. I love my family more passionately. I love opportunities to serve more fervently. And I imagine more audaciously.

Max De Pree has written, "Leaders are like small boys at the end of summer."[5] Small boys at the end of summer are all nicked and bruised, sunburned and bloodied, but unbowed and always ready for more. Show me to the future! Give me something to live for, to believe in, and to fight for! I want to live audaciously!

Part Three
Reflection Questions

1. Practice the discipline of imagining audaciously. What would you imagine for yourself and others that would move you on a fulfillment scale toward a *TEN*?

2. Based on the dream God gave him, Jacob imagined a new reality and articulated it into the branches. Where could you articulate a new reality? Would it be a mission statement for your family, business, or nonprofit? A plan for your continuing education? A plan to achieve financial independence?

3. What type of conversations do you have with yourself? Do you self-prophesy negative or positive thoughts? How would you change your self-talk to reflect your aspirations for a life that's a *TEN*?

4. What do you speak to the people around you? How would you change your language toward others to convey your faith in them and their ability to move their lives towards a *TEN* and to live out their best destiny?

Part Four

GROW

Chapter 14

Not Always This Way

ABRAHAM LINCOLN WAS AN incredibly ambitious man. Lincoln was also humble. His insatiable appetite to achieve great things drove him to the full development of himself, particularly his character. There was not necessarily anything innately extraordinary about Lincoln. He wasn't born with particularly good looks, a charming personality, an educated mind, or polished leadership skills. What he was born with, however, was an impenetrable drive to become the best man he could be.

"Every man is said to have his peculiar ambition," the twenty-three-year-old Abraham Lincoln wrote in his open letter to the people during his first bid for public office. "I have no other [ambition] so great as that of being truly esteemed of my fellow men, by rendering myself worthy of their esteem."[1] The ambition to establish a reputation so that his story could be told after his death had carried Lincoln through his bleak childhood, his laborious efforts to educate himself, his string of political failures, and a depression so profound that he declared himself more than willing to die. The ambition he had for his future was his motivation to develop himself.

Abraham Lincoln was well over six feet tall. He was even bigger on the inside. In 1908, Tolstoy, one of the greatest thinkers and writers of his time, poignantly described Lincoln as "bigger than his country...bigger than all the Presidents together."[2]

But Lincoln wasn't always this way.

Few people are acquainted with the Blackhawk War, a series of skirmishes between the United States and two Indian tribes in 1832. During this relatively inconspicuous conflict, Lincoln was commissioned to serve as a captain. He was quickly discovered to have less than stellar leadership skills. On one distinct occasion, the future president of the United States led his company through a field where they encountered a fence. He couldn't determine the proper command to get his men through an opening in the fence in an orderly fashion. At a complete loss, he had them "fall out" for a few minutes and reassemble on the other side. He had trouble just getting his men through a simple roadblock in a field!

At this stage of Lincoln's development, some of his men described him as "indolent and vulgar." Others regarded him as "a joke, an absurdity, and had serious doubts about his courage." They said, "Any old woman would have made a more credible commander than he did."[3] When his company was disbanded at the end of the war, Abraham Lincoln had been demoted to private.

Years later, President Lincoln was a skilled commander in chief guiding his country through one of the darkest periods in its history with legendary leadership skills. So, what happened? What caused Lincoln to metamorphose from a failed military captain into, arguably, the greatest leader in the history of the nation? This monumental change can be attributed to one thing: he grew. Lincoln knew he had to align his emotional, mental, and spiritual realities with his dreams of greatness.

For many years, Lincoln had gotten up early, stayed up late, read voraciously, studied fervently, grappled with issues, honed his arguments, cared deeply, and spent time with others who helped expand his understanding: "His desire for understanding had almost become a passion . . . He watched what went on about him . . . and did a great deal of thinking. In his leisure time at home and on the circuit he read the newspapers assiduously . . . he was never satisfied handling a thought until, as he said, he had bounded it east, west, north and south and could express it in the simplest, clearest language."[4]

He became multi-dimensional in his development by mastering a diversity of disciplines, including the teachings of the Bible, the mathematics of Euclid, and the classics like Shakespeare. This unquenchable passion to accomplish his fullest development allowed him to create preferred futures for countless millions.

Nobody knows *everything* they need to know.

—Dave Marcum, Steve Smith, Mahan Khalsa,
Business Think[5]

Even when I was a teenager, I was ambitious to do great things. Though ambition is not inherently negative, I know my motives weren't entirely pure. My drive to succeed had to be refined so that I wanted the right things for the right reasons. I am still in this process. As Jeremiah advised a young colleague named Baruch, "Should you then seek great things for yourself? Seek them not" (Jer. 45:5).

We've all experienced painful growth moments. I think of times when I came to sobering realizations that there would be some major repercussions if I didn't change in some way, grow in some area, or develop some part of my character more fully. I knew that even God-inspired dreams for my life, my family, and the church I served would never be fulfilled if I didn't grow.

I can remember as a very young man becoming aware that other people viewed me as talented yet cocky. A deep recognition of my need to humble myself before God became a central focus in my life. I remember another time when I came to understand that as a leader and as a husband I desperately needed to learn what it meant to be a servant. I came to the conclusion that if I didn't learn servanthood, my relationships with the people most important to me would end up being broken. I can also remember coming to the realization that to build a winning and spiritually connected team, I had to be fully engaged in caring for the holistic health of my teammates. I had to share power. Give others the credit. Not be intimidated as I surrounded myself with people more talented than I am. Those are just a few examples of development I have experienced as a person and as a leader. I still have much more growing to do.

The greater our God-inspired ambitions, the greater is our need to develop the life infrastructure necessary to sustain them. An infrastructure can be described as a substructure or underlying foundation. Our life infrastructure has to do with our spiritual formation, the building of our character, the shaping of our attitude, the gaining of knowledge, and learning to apply all of this to our lives through wisdom. It pertains to the things that lie beneath the surface of our lives but provide the foundation for everything else.

Here is an incredibly important concept. We've already learned in this book that God has destined beyond-imagination futures that are for our and others' benefit. We discussed how 1 Corinthians 2 teaches, "No eye has seen, no ear has heard, and no mind has imagined what God has prepared for those who love him. But we know these things because God has revealed them to us by his Spirit, and his Spirit searches out everything and shows us even God's deep secrets" (vv. 9–10, NLT).

That's the good news.

But Paul then continues this thought: "Dear brothers and sisters, when I was with you I couldn't talk to you as I would to mature Christians. I had to talk as though you belonged to this world or as though you were infants in the Christian life. I had to feed you with milk and not with solid food, because you couldn't handle anything stronger. And you still aren't ready" (1 Cor. 3:1–2, NLT).

That's the bad news.

The good news was that God had tremendous plans for the Corinthians. The bad news was that Paul couldn't even talk to them about these plans— as he would have liked—because they weren't ready for them. He goes on to complain about their high level of immaturity and gets specific about areas in which they had to be more fully developed as a church and as individuals in order for God's dreams for them to come true. What a lesson for all of us! All the audacious imaginings in the world will not bring about preferred futures unless we are supported by a life infrastructure that He can work within.

Chapter 15
Theory Y God

DOUGLAS MCGREGOR, A BUSINESS theorist and important influencer of management practices, introduced a much-discussed philosophy of management. He believed that managers manage according to their particular assumptions about human nature. As a result, he developed the Theory X and Theory Y concept, juxtaposing two management styles.

A Theory X manager basically believes most people are really unmotivated and aren't willing to put forth the effort to reach their potential. Consequently, according to a Theory X manager, people have to be very closely controlled in order for them to accomplish anything beneficial. McGregor conceptualized Theory X as follows:

- Work is inherently distasteful to most people.

- Most people are not ambitious, have little desire for responsibility, and prefer to be directed.

- Most people have little capacity for creativity in solving organizational problems.

- Motivation occurs only at the physiological and security levels.

- Most people must be closely controlled and often coerced to achieve organizational objectives.[1]

Theory Y is the opposing management construct he developed. McGregor concluded that Theory Y managers assume people have a desire to excel, possess the capability to be self-motivated, and want their work to be meaningful and about more than just a paycheck. Theory Y managers, then, have the following paradigm:

- Work is as natural as play, if the conditions are favorable.

- Self-control is often indispensable in achieving organizational goals.

- The capacity for creativity in solving organization problems is widely distributed in the population.

- Motivation occurs at the social, esteem, and self-actualization levels, as well as at the physiological and security levels.

- People can be self-directed and creative at work if properly motivated.[2]

In the popular text *Management of Organizational Behavior,* the assertion is made that, "Managers may have Theory Y assumptions about human nature, but they may find it necessary to behave in a very directive, controlling manner (as if they had Theory X assumptions) with some people in the short run to help them 'grow up' in a developmental sense until they are truly Theory Y–acting people."[3] When I read this statement a few years ago, I was intensely impacted by this thought: God is a Theory Y God. He created us in His image. He alone knows how much potential we really have. He has great plans for us. Sometimes, though, sadly, He has to manage us in Theory X ways until we "grow up." Only then can His dreams for us be realized by us.

In the Bible, we are challenged to become mature, so we will "no longer be infants" but "in all things grow up" into Christ (Eph. 4:14–15). During a recent study break, my wife, Sharon, and I were able to spend a great deal of time talking openly with each other about our perspective of the other's growth. It was dangerous but fruitful.

A family in our congregation had loaned us their beautiful home in Maine on a pristine inlet just off the Atlantic. Over several days, we each read all or parts of Peter Scazzero's books about the connection between authentic spirituality and emotional health.[4] We each took a lengthy self-assessment that identified different levels of emotional maturity. The survey charted one's development in several areas as to whether one is an emotional infant, child, adolescent, or adult. Finally, we gave the other permission to challenge our self-assessment by talking through our answers to each question.

We spent hours on this exercise. One reason it took so long was that there were several hours during that day when we didn't speak to each other at all! But with twenty-three years of marriage as a backdrop, we worked through the pain of each other's honesty and grew from the experience. Just for the record, we are now at twenty-nine years and counting.

This exercise demonstrates a practical means that I used to identify some areas in which I need to "grow up." We all have multiple areas in our lives where we need to grow. We must realize how high the stakes are. God cannot speak to us about preferred futures unless we grow up. We must become bigger people. We must be willing to expand as human beings in order to become the persons that God sees us capable of becoming. And the more ambitious we are, the more we must be willing to fully develop ourselves in every dimension of our lives.

In the 1940s, psychologist Abraham Maslow coined the term "self-actualization." He defined it as the highest state of being a human could experience. He theorized that as humans meet basic needs, such as physiological and security needs, they seek to satisfy successively higher needs, the highest being self-actualization. Self-actualized persons are, among other things, "relatively free of delusion...not constrained by fear of what others will think of them...more tolerant of themselves and others...have a consuming mission in life involving wide philosophical or ethical issues.... They live rich, emotional lives and...have deep sympathy for their fellow human beings and a strong desire to help others."[5]

I like to talk about becoming God-actualized, where who we are in every way is fully matured so we can actually live out our God-given potential. What would it mean to "become mature, attaining to the whole measure of the fullness of Christ" (Eph. 4:13)? Jesus Christ, "the image of the invisible God" (Col. 1:15), was obviously the most actualized human being who ever lived. What would it really be like to have Him fully formed in our lives?

I've made a conscious effort to be around people who are bigger than I am—those who I believe are more God-actualized in certain areas of their lives than I:

- People who don't sweat the small stuff.

- People who don't become angry quickly.

- People who are tremendously bright but deeply humble.

- People who are not easily offended and can easily forgive.

- People who work hard and play harder.

- People who get up early, stay up late, accomplish much, and sleep soundly.

- People who have been in the game for a long time and have kept their integrity.

- People who have suffered yet still exude joy.

- People who have risked much and are willing to sacrifice for even more.

I think about a mentor of mine who has experienced tremendous success in his field. He was married over fifty years; his wife has since passed away. I simply remember how, in ways great and small, he honored his wife and was profoundly kind to her. That impacted me.

Another leader comes to mind, a man I've spent years listening to, reading after, and who I recently got to know. He is extremely intelligent, but not just because he has a high IQ. He reads broadly, he studies thoroughly, he thinks long and hard about what and how to communicate, and he always communicates well. I'm inspired by that.

I also have a friend who is a recovering alcoholic. Years ago, he came back from the abyss. Many years sober, he works the Twelve Steps every day—one step a week—year after year. He faithfully practices principles like taking a moral inventory and making things right with those he's harmed. There are times I feel dwarfed by his internal bigness. He lives deep. He knows he has to, to survive. But really we all have to—to survive and succeed. I need to be around people like this.

Being around people who are big, and especially those whose bigness reflects Christ, challenges me to work on the infrastructure of my life.

I want to espouse the type of mature greatness that flows from the depths of a person, as well as the development of the aptitudes associated with it. Nobody wakes up and just is a deep person. You must work hard to become aware of your blind spots and work on your weaknesses. Why am I feeling what I'm feeling? Why did I make that decision? Why am I ambitious for that certain thing? Though it can be quite an arduous process, if you have audacious imaginings about your preferred future, you must grow.

Superficiality is the curse of our age.

—Richard Foster,
Celebration of Discipline[6]

Do you want to be great? Do you want to be a leader? Do you want to build preferred futures? To build the infrastructure necessary for success, we have to:

- pray, to know God and ourselves;
- learn to lead ourselves;
- expand our knowledge about things beyond ourselves;
- keep doing the right things regardless of results; and
- have a proper understanding of success.

I want to spend the remainder of this section exploring some of these opportunities for personal growth.

Chapter 16
Know Thyself

THE PRACTICE OF PRAYER is the most important aspect of my ongoing spiritual development—especially the type of prayer that seeks to know God for the sake of knowing Him. It's in this context that one also most fully comes to know one's self. By establishing an intimate relationship with God, we are subconsciously following Socrates' admonishment to "know thyself."

John Calvin wrote, "Our wisdom, in so far as it ought to be deemed true and solid wisdom, consists almost entirely of two parts: the knowledge of God and of ourselves. But as these are connected together by many ties, it is not easy to determine which of the two precedes, and gives birth to the other."[1]

St. Augustine prayed, "Grant Lord, that I may know myself that I may know Thee."[2]

There are many ways of praying, but the kind of prayer I am specifically advocating in this context is contemplative prayer. The most important methodology in this prayer is to simply be alone. Alone. Just you and God. Talking. Listening. Contemplating. Meditating. Thinking. As Blaise Pascal wisely wrote, "All men's miseries derive from not being able to sit in a quiet room alone."[3] When we spend time alone with God, we become more conscious of His presence and His thoughts and ourselves and our thoughts. We are, therefore, expanding in the depths of our spirit-selves.

The only way to learn this is by practicing. We have to learn how to talk with God and somehow, in a way I cannot fully explain or even understand, listen to God. Not for an audible voice, but for that inexplicable awareness that the Spirit of God is communicating into our spirit.

Frequently, people will approach me with much frustration and say, "Pastor Terry, I don't know how to pray." And I'll reply, "Well, just say that to God." They will usually look at me kind of embarrassed but inquisitively and announce, "God, I don't know how to pray," to which I respond, "Congratulations! You just prayed!"

Don't overcomplicate prayer. You don't have to approach God with a certain kind of voice, using "thees" and "thous," or having your life perfectly in order. In fact, spending time knowing Him in this manner is the avenue to allow Him to help you straighten out the crooked areas in your life.

"To pray," Emilie Griffin writes, "means willing to be naïve."[4]

> I used to think that I needed to get all my motives straightened out before I could pray, really pray. . . . The truth of the matter is, we all come to prayer with a tangled mass of motives—altruistic *and* selfish, merciful *and* hateful, loving *and* bitter. Frankly, this side of eternity we will *never* unravel the good from the bad, the pure from the impure. But what I have come to see is that God is big enough to receive us with all our mixture. We do not have to be bright, or pure, or filled with faith, or anything. . . . We will never have pure enough motives, or be good enough, or know enough in order to pray rightly. We simply must set all these things aside and begin praying. In fact, it is in the very act of prayer itself—the intimate, ongoing interaction with God—that these matters are cared for in due time.[5]

There's a difference between knowing about God and knowing Him. Later, I will discuss the importance of study. Nevertheless, the most important "thing" to study is God. We should study Him through the Bible.

Through our relationships. Through nature. But the most essential way to study God is through our own relationship with Him.

There's a great story about A. W. Tozer, who is probably most famous for writing the spiritual classic *The Pursuit of God*. He was giving advice to Cliff Westergren, a young man who was preparing to begin theological studies. Tozer said, "My son, when you get to college you're going to find that all of the boys will be gathered in a room discussing and arguing over Arminianism and Calvinism night after night after night. I'll tell you what to do, Cliff. Go to your room and meet God and at the end of four years, you'll be way down the line and they'll still be where they started, because greater minds than yours have wrestled with this problem and have not come up with satisfactory conclusions. Instead, learn to know God."[6]

A *Harvard Business Review* article examined the difficulty most leaders have in maintaining a capacity for reflection and making sound decisions in a high-stress, chaotic environment. The article included a metaphor which comes to my mind when I think about contemplative prayer: "Get off the dance floor and onto the balcony."[7] The dance floor is that noisy, constantly moving, trying-to-keep-up-with-everything place in our lives. The balcony is the place where we can look down, even on ourselves, and gain perspective and clarity about our lives.

Prayer, for me, is going up to the balcony. It's the place where I experience solitude and quiet in His presence. The place where I ask God questions. The place where I listen. The place where I contemplate my own life. Why do I feel the way I do about that situation? What decision should I make? Why did I experience that conflict? I think about my life, my place, and my future while in the presence of God.

In the Old Testament, Joshua and his army made a mistake that cost the country of Israel dearly because they didn't "inquire of the Lord" (Josh. 1:14). It is incredible for me to think that I can ask God for advice and expect to be able to "hear" Him. Communication is more about learning to listen than it is about learning to talk. As Stephen Covey told us, we must "seek first to understand, then to be understood."[8]

A number of years ago, I toured Winston Churchill's Cabinet War Rooms in London. Far underneath the ground in that city, there was a labyrinth of tunnels which connected a myriad of rooms. During WWII, Churchill and other significant leaders assembled in this underground infrastructure—safe from the bombing—to strategize, make crucial decisions, and generate wartime plans. There was also a spartan area where Churchill could refresh himself and rest. To excavate the depths of God's presence and gain His wisdom for our lives, we must remove ourselves from life's overwhelming pandemonium, the distracting noises, the conflicting voices, and the committees in our head.

I've advocated our capacity to "draw a circle" around certain areas of our world in which we can make a difference. The first circle we must draw is around ourselves. We must not only know ourselves, but we must practice self-control. We must accept responsibility for our own growth. Daniel Goleman in his insightful book *Emotional Intelligence* wrote, "Exceptional leaders distinguish themselves because of superior self-leadership."[9]

When I think about self-awareness and self-leadership, I reflect on our need to manage emotions and leverage our impulses toward positive ends. For me, it's quite clear that the first key to this is to cultivate the life of the Spirit. Goleman explored "the eternal battle between impulse and restraint, id and ego, desire and self-control, gratification and delay."[10] The apostle Paul talked about the battle between the "flesh," or the "sinful nature", and the "Spirit": "So I say, live by the Spirit, and you will not gratify the desires of the sinful nature" (Gal. 5:16). The Message states it like this: "These two ways of life are antithetical, so that you cannot live at times one way and at times another way according to how we feel on any given day. Why don't you choose to be led by the Spirit?" The "works of the flesh"—reacting to our base, human emotions or impulses—are self- and others-destructive! The "fruit of the spirit," however, or what the Spirit produces in our lives, is "love, joy, peace, patience, kindness, goodness, faithfulness, gentleness, and self control" (Gal. 5:22–23).

I like to say that the "fruit of the spirit" is emotional intelligence.

According to this passage in Galatians 5, emotional intelligence cannot be experienced by living according to our human impulses or by attempting to keep a set of religious rules. The secret is fostering the life of the Spirit. Our first objective, then, is not to say, "I have to be self-controlled" but rather, "I have to cultivate the life of the Spirit." As our spiritual lives are nurtured, the energies of the Spirit work in us toward the development of self-leadership. Eugene Peterson says self-control is being "able to marshal and direct our energies wisely" (Gal. 5:23, MSG).

We can't sit around and wait for other people to plan our lives for us. We can't be idle and hope some corporation, our parents, or our future spouse is going to pave the way to our future. We have to own it, to manage it, to develop it. No one is going to seize opportunities for me but me. No one can nurture your spiritual life for you but you.

With the force of the Spirit at work, we can begin to lead ourselves toward the expansion of many life skills. We are responsible for ourselves. We are responsible to invite God's presence into our lives. We are responsible for our thoughts, our feelings, and our actions. We have a will. We make decisions. We reap what we sow. We must know ourselves and lead ourselves to our preferred futures.

Chapter 17
Learn

More and more people in the workforce—and most knowledge workers—will have to manage themselves. They will have to place themselves where they can make the greatest contribution; they will have to learn to develop themselves.... They will have to learn how and when to change what they do, how they do it and when they do it.

—Peter Drucker,
Management Challenges for the 21st Century[1]

To seize the opportunity of a rapidly changing world, we must see the full development of ourselves as a constant need and privilege. We must regularly increase our knowledge, our competence, our skills, and our interests. Education should be a way of life, preparing us to live to the fullest extent of our potential.

Growing people make learning intentional: "Principle-centered people are constantly educated by their experiences. They read, they seek training, they take classes, they listen to others, they learn through both their ears and their eyes.... They discover that the more they know, the more they realize they don't know."[2] It amazes me how many people quit actively pursuing learning when they finish the formal educational process. Mark McCormack, the pioneer of sports marketing and author of *What They Don't Teach You in Harvard Business School*, commented, "An education, as part of the ongoing learning process, is at best a foundation and at worst a naïve form of arrogance. The best lesson anyone can learn from business school is an awareness of what it can't teach you—all the ins and outs of everyday business life. Those ins and outs are largely a self-learning process."[3]

This is what we all need. I call it the utility of humility. Learners approach life with an attitude of humility; they understand how much they don't know. The authors of the book *Business Think* explored the reasons behind failed business decisions and failed businesses. They determined that over 50 percent of business decisions are bad decisions. They discovered that 82 percent of businesses go under before their tenth anniversary and that eight out of ten new products fail. Yet their data shows that 91 percent of business leaders are highly confident in their ability to make good decisions.[4]

Why? What is the solution to this troubling information? These experts formed seven rules to counter the grim reality of these negative statistics. Their first rule was: "Check your ego at the door." The second rule was: "Create curiosity." The segue between these two rules was that "nobody knows everything they need to know to make crucial decisions in something as complex as business...The cure for ego is humility...Contrary to popular belief, humility is not a weakness. In fact, by our definition humility is incredibly powerful."[5]

We hired architect David Price to design our new church campus. David is nothing less than brilliant. His architectural degree is from Harvard University. He studied art in Italy. His father, Buzz Price, was one of Walt Disney's confidants and one of the creators of Disneyland and Walt Disney World. David brings a lot of unique experiences and knowledge to his work. When we were working on the initial stages of this design, we had a meeting with some of the stakeholders in our community, including the mayor, the township attorney, planning officials, and others. We wanted their insight early in the process as to how our new campus would impact the community.

David made a tremendous presentation, articulately describing his vision. He then subjected himself to a multitude of questions from this wide variety of people. Some questions were a bit elementary in light of David's broad knowledge of planning, architecture, and his inspired ideas. But David stood there smiling, engaging in the appropriate dialogue, establishing a genuine rapport, and answering all of their questions as if he had all the time in the world. After the meeting was adjourned, I thanked him for his willing cooperation and patience. I'll never forget how he responded: "What a good architect needs is a sense of humility."

David wasn't just answering questions. He was simultaneously listening and finding out about the community. He wasn't just teaching; he was also learning. Lifelong learners approach every situation with humility and see it as an opportunity to expand their own base of competence.

I was struck by an article that chronicled the dangers of the absence of doubt and a "grandiose sense of self-importance."[6] It is probably evident, by now, that I am a faith guy. I'm easily able to visualize preferred futures, but I have come to understand that, paradoxically, I have to utilize a humility that acknowledges a healthy degree of self-doubt. Not God-doubt, self-doubt. I have to do due diligence. I have to seek wise counsel. I have to carefully form well-considered strategies and plans. I have to make sure that I am learning what I need to know in order to be successful.

Sometimes the need to learn new things in order to create preferred futures can involve risk, sacrifice, and a readjustment of our lives. Russ Hammonds has a degree in physics from Brown University, but his dream is to create preferred futures through the arts. His passionate desire is to write spirituality-infused television and movie scripts to positively impact the cultural morass. Even in light of his Ivy League degree, he had to shift his focus and energies and start creating his preferred future from scratch. Russ began managing a talent agency and studying his chosen art voraciously. In order to fully grasp a faith-based worldview, he read many spiritual classics, including nearly everything written by C. S. Lewis. Russ now spends hours each day writing while working on a television show full time as a post-production supervisor.

Maria Rice Bellamy, who has a degree in economics from Harvard University, has a dream to create preferred futures through academia. While she could be earning a high salary working in the financial world, she believes God has different dreams for her. Maria went on to study at Oxford and earned a master's degree in literature. She invested six years of her life to earn a PhD and now serves as an assistant professor at the College of Staten Island. I watched her make many sacrifices during this time—working part-time on the church staff at far less than market value, driving an old jalopy of a car, and finding the time in her extraordinarily busy schedule to study, write her dissertation, and teach undergraduates at Rutgers University.

Matt Epperson and his family made some major readjustments when he shifted his vocational focus toward what he believed was God's vision for his life. Equipped with a master's degree in social work, Matt held a prominent position in a North Carolina county mental health organization. Although he had always had a compelling desire to be involved in social justice matters, his job at that time was too politically oriented within the organization and Matt wasn't getting to do what he really loved. He had no opportunities to get his hands dirty and work with the actual people in need in order to make the differences he felt he was called to make.

Matt believed God wanted him to go back to school so he could eventually educate people about the social issues that are shaping our society. Within one year, he had moved his family from the South to New Jersey so he could pursue his PhD at Columbia University. Now? He has finished his work at Columbia and is an assistant professor at the University of Chicago.

Characteristic of Matt and his wife's "untraveled-path" mentality, this Caucasian family—who already had three other children—adopted an African American baby during this hectic period in their lives. Though they have made many financial and comfort sacrifices, they were, and still are, willing to do the unusual because they are constantly expanding inside, and they are people who are always wanting more.

Chapter 18
Keep Doing the Right Things

Struggle is not fun. But it is better than fun.

—Richard Nixon,
In the Arena[1]

WHEN THE NEW YORK Yankees won the World Championship in 1998, they marked their season campaign by breaking the record for the most wins (125) of any team in any season in baseball history. Pitcher Andy Pettitte won the eighty-ninth game of this historic season against the Texas Rangers. In the seventh inning of this game, the Yankees were ahead 3–1 when Pettitte walked lead-off hitter Juan Gonzalez.

Will Clark hit a blooper between shortstop Derek Jeter and center-fielder Bernie Williams. They ran toward each other, each trying to catch it, but the ball dropped. Williams picked it up. As Pettitte's heart sank, he saw Tino Martinez, the Yankees' first baseman, yelling for the ball at second base. In a split second, Williams realized the batter was halfway to second and threw it to Martinez for a pivotal out. That ended the inning and ultimately clinched the Yankees' victory.

This fundamentally sound play by Martinez is an example of what it means to do the right thing over and over, regardless of an immediate payoff: "He had run this route hundreds of times in his career, just in case he was needed—and last night was the first time he could remember making an out as a result."[2]

Martinez had repeatedly run from his position at first base in order to cover second base on similar blips to the outfield. It was tedious. It was boring. But it was the right thing to do even when, hundreds of times before, it never resulted in an out. One play on this one night influenced the outcome for one win that moved the Yankees toward perhaps the most successful season in baseball history.

Here's the point: Keep going to second base. Keep doing the fundamentally right things regardless of whether or not they immediately pay off. There's a lot to be said about getting up every day and doing these things until at some point over time, we experience a victorious result. Great dreams, ideas, and futures don't happen overnight; they unravel through perseverance.

As you move toward your preferred future, there will be times when your ideas work and times when your ideas fail. There will be times when you experience good days and times when you suffer bad days. There will be times in your new business when your profit margins are really high and times when you wonder whether or not you are going to survive. Don't lose hope! People who keep getting up every day, who keep growing, who keep learning, and who keep praying are ultimately going to keep winning.

In the New Testament, James reminds us to mimic the farmer who patiently waits for the harvest and does not grumble (Jas. 5:7–9). This can be a problem for me. When I have a dream and plant a seed, sometimes I find myself immediately standing over it, stomping the ground, and yelling, "C'mon seed! Grow!" But I am learning that I must have patience while the seed is in the ground. People who create preferred futures are long-suffering, not complainers, whiners, or overly anxious.

I read a story about the influential president of a major Japanese company who was answering questions from a businesswoman. At that time, his company was flourishing in an extraordinary way.

Question: "Mr. President, does your company have long-range goals?"
Answer: "Yes."
Question: "How long are your long-range goals?"
Answer: "Two hundred fifty years."
Question: "What do you need to carry them out?"
Answer: "Patience."[3]

The founder of Wal-Mart, Sam Walton, detailed a similar, though shorter, success time frame in his autobiography: "The first Wal-Mart store was a sensational success. But it wasn't an overnight success like some people think it was. It was a success twenty years in the making."[4] Walton started his retail journey with a little dime store and through the years experimented with different types of ideas, some of which worked and others that didn't. He did this for years, and then he finally got the formula right. Success is a habit!

A lot of people give up on their dreams too quickly. Part of being successful is simply sticking around long enough, doing the right things over and over, and nurturing a life environment that allows God, who makes things grow (2 Cor. 3:6), to show up and make dreams come true. We must persevere!

You can't sustain excellence if you vacillate. In any business there are natural ebbs and flows.

—Bill Parcells,
Finding a Way to Win[5]

What is success anyway?

Success is the process of accomplishing those things for which we were destined in a way that honors God, loves people, and brings joy.

In the best-seller *Into Thin Air*, Jon Krakauer weaves a riveting firsthand account of the 1996 expedition to the summit of Mount Everest. This highest point on the earth reaches a staggering 29,028 feet. To date, there have been an estimated 1,924 ascents and 179 deaths.

During the 1996 climbing season, nineteen people—including two of Krakauer's close friends—died trying to conquer this mountain. He made it. This is what he said about reaching the summit:

> Straddling the top of the world, one foot in China and the other in Nepal, I cleared the ice from my oxygen mask, hunched a shoulder against the wind, and stared absently down at the vastness of Tibet. . . . Now that I was finally here, actually standing on the summit of Mount Everest, I just couldn't summon the energy to care. . . . I hadn't slept in fifty-seven hours. The only food I'd been able to force down over the preceding three days was a bowl of ramen soup and a handful of peanut M&Ms. . . . Under the circumstances, I was incapable of feeling much of anything except cold and tired. . . . I snapped four quick photos . . . then turned and headed down. . . . All told, I'd spent less than five minutes on the roof of the world.[6]

After investing years in training and three months climbing in the worst possible conditions, Krakauer stood at the top of the world. But you know what? He was at the summit for five minutes and was too exhausted to enjoy it! Success is not the eventual achievement of our dreams or desires; it's the process of accomplishing those things.

Krakauer talked about the joy he found in climbing the mountain. He called the process the "unfettered pleasures of ascent."[7] His triumph was experienced not only through reaching the summit, but in the slow climb toward the achievement of his goal.

Most of our lives could be described as a continual ascent to some distant summit. Most human beings have an innate desire to attain the highest possibilities of life. I use the word *innate* intentionally, for this passion for the apex—this quest for the heights—seems to just be in us. But it is the journey to our futures that yields the greatest rewards.

Dr. Les Parrott, professor of psychology at Seattle Pacific University, offered three key markers to mental health. The first two are having a sense of meaning and purpose and a capacity for personal responsibility.

Parrott's third marker particularly challenged me, though: "A person must be willing to be happy in the present."[8] He defined psychological health as a sense of well-being and a willingness to be involved in the process. He then quoted Abraham Maslow: "Some people spend their entire lives indefinitely preparing to live."

Some of us are spending our lives preparing for life. We're waiting for someday or for when this dream comes true...that business gets started...my kids graduate college...I pay off my debt...I retire. Someday. When? In order for us to really be growing people, we can't forget that as we're working on better, best, and preferred things, we still must show up in the present and be thankful for this moment. That's now. Today. This very moment.

Bob Wieland was a big part of an effort early in my ministry to impact young people with a message of faith, values, and success. Bob was a strapping 6'2" athlete on his way toward a promising career in major league baseball when he was drafted into the army. On his second day in Vietnam, he stepped on a mortar while trying to save a fellow soldier. Bob's legs went one direction, his body another.

When I met Bob, he stood just 2'10" tall. But he was a huge man. I remember being with him in Milwaukee as we prepared to speak to hundreds of young people at his former high school. We stood on the field where he played baseball, which is now named Bob Wieland Field. His message was that, despite the obstacles and challenges life may present, you can always find a way to win.

In the weeks and months that followed Bob's losing his legs, he battled severe depression and a desire to commit suicide. But through faith in God, Bob found an overwhelming sense of purpose. In time, Bob became a strong advocate for physical fitness and broke various weightlifting records, including the world record for the bench press. He served on the President's Council on Physical Fitness and Sports. He completed the New York, Los Angeles, and Marine Corps marathons and became the strength and motivation coach for the Green Bay Packers. Among many accolades he has received, in 1996 Bob was named "The Most Courageous Man in America" by the NFL Players Association.

Perhaps his most significant achievement was when he championed the Walk for Hunger organization by walking across America—on his hands. Bob propels himself by lifting and pushing his body forward with his powerful arms. On September 8, 1982, in Orange County, California, Bob began this three-year, eight-month, six-day odyssey of walking 2,800 miles across the country. He relied on hand grips that acted as shoes, creams to soothe his blistering skin, and leather chaps that covered his seat and what is left of his legs. Averaging a pace of three to five miles a day, Bob successfully completed his goal at the Vietnam War Memorial in Washington, DC, on May 14, 1986. Greeted by a mass of media, loyal supporters, and Vietnam veterans, he placed a wreath by the name of the man he was trying to save when he lost his legs.

President Ronald Reagan welcomed Bob into the Oval Office before he completed his final mile. I remember Bob telling me what he had asked the nation's leader: "Mr. President, when was the last time someone walked 4,900,016 steps on his hands just to say hello to you?"

Bob has often said that his greatest triumph was not being welcomed by his fellow veterans or even the president of the United States, but that "the joy was in the journey." While I've heard this statement many times over many years, it always has special meaning when I hear it from Bob.

This book is about creating a preferred future—one that does not presently exist. Yet we must not forget the need to be full of gratitude, joy, and love right now.

We must always be aware of the "unfettered pleasures of ascent."

Want more. But be content. Tomorrow we're expecting something better, but today is a great day.

Part Four

Reflection Questions

1. Consider this thought: "The greater our God-inspired ambitions, the greater our need to develop the infrastructure to sustain them." What does this mean to you? What can you do to stimulate growth to support God's dreams for your life?

2. Are there things God has planned for your life that He's not able to do because you need to grow up? What are some of those under-developed areas of your life? What do you need to do to stimulate growth in that area?

3. How might fostering your spiritual life help you to know yourself and gain emotional intelligence? What are the practical implications of the statement, "Emotional intelligence is the fruit of the Spirit"? What could you do to cultivate the life of the Spirit?

4. Consider this: "Success is the process of accomplishing those things for which we were destined in a way that honors God, loves people, and brings joy." What can you do along the path to your best destiny to remind yourself that *TEN* is not just achieving a goal, but also the fulfillment experienced in the process of achieving that goal?

Part Five

ACT

Chapter 19

Be an Actor

PEOPLE IN WEST ORANGE call him "Baba" with great affection. His real name is Emmanuel Anim-Sackey. Emmanuel is an actor. Not on the screen or stage but in life. He was raised in Abetifi-Kwahu, Ghana, and immigrated to the United States in 1996. He worked hard to secure a job as a US postal worker—an incredibly rich job for a guy from Abetifi-Kwahu. Saddled with what felt to him like incredible prosperity, he started thinking about his people back in Ghana. Many of them live without shoes, decent clothing, or basic health care. Children walk for miles, often in the dark, through dangerous jungle to attend a poorly functioning school in a dilapidated building.

Baba decided that he could feel guilty for being "rich" or he could do something. So he began going to yard and garage sales and buying used clothing and other goods. When he would travel to Ghana, he would take everything he could carry with him and then distribute it to people in his village according to their needs. Then people on his postal route found out. Here was this incredibly competent man with an infectious smile spending all his spare time and money to serve his people back in Ghana.

A movement began. Household after household began giving their used clothing to Emmanuel. The community of West Orange adopted Abetifi-Kwahu as a sister village. A nonprofit called Adopt One Village was started. A local developer donated the use of a warehouse to share the overwhelming quantity of donations that began to come in. Clothing.

Hospital beds. Bicycles. Medical equipment. Furniture. Computers. Sports equipment. Books. Emmanuel started shipping cargo containers to Abetifi-Kwahu. Everybody got involved. Jews. Christians. Muslims. Because Baba decided to act.

The first time I remember meeting Emmanuel was in the lobby of our church one weekend. He introduced himself and said that he wanted to invite me to the mayor's annual State of the Town address. He said he was being recognized for his work in Ghana. I was able to see him awarded the Citizen of the Year award in West Orange. Then the following year, amazingly, he was awarded the Humanitarian of the Year award for the US Postal Service. I get to be his pastor.

This past year, our church had two missions to Abetifi-Kwahu. We rebuilt the medical center, provided basic medical care, and distributed three shipping containers of goods, including 150 bicycles so kids could ride to school instead of walking long distances in the dark on bare feet. This year we're sending hundreds of pairs of shoes!

All because Emmanuel decided to be an actor. He had a picture of a God-inspired future, but it wasn't enough to leave it at that. He had to actualize it. God doesn't come down and show up just because we have a dream and are waiting for it to materialize out of thin air. God typically chooses people who have, in some way, given Him something to work with. We have to act!

Even Mary, the mother of Jesus, had to participate with God in order to give birth to a miracle. I see her story as a model for creating God's preferred future. There are five things I observe in how her will and actions allowed her to connect with God's plan for her life and, more importantly, His world.

First, she was willing to wonder. When the angel showed up to give Mary the message from God about the unique role she was about to play in the human story, she "was greatly troubled at his words and wondered" (Luke 1:29). I think that we often focus on her being "troubled" or frightened. Of course she was freaked out! She was a young teenager visited by God. But thankfully, she was also full of wonder. Eugene Peterson writes: "Wonder is the only adequate launching pad for exploring a spirituality of creation, keeping us open-eyed, expectant, alive to life that is always more than we can account for, that always exceeds our calculations, that is always beyond anything we can make."[1] Mary wondered. She opened to possibility.

Second, she was willing to hear. She listened as the angel told her about God's choice to use her to usher in a new age. She sought clarity, she asked questions, but she listened. "How will this be," Mary asked the angel, "since I am a virgin?" (Luke 1:34). The angel said, "God is going to do this thing in you. God is going to cause you to conceive. I know that this seems impossible, but 'nothing is impossible with God'" (vv. 35–37, AUTHOR'S PARAPHRASE).

Third, she was willing to say yes to God's dream for her. "I am the Lord's servant," Mary answered. "May it be to me as you have said" (v. 38). She activated her will to agree with her God destiny. I believe that this is when she conceived God's Son. She had to say, "Yes."

Fourth, Mary was willing to be pregnant with the future. I think the most difficult time for a miracle is the time of gestation. The time when we know God has put something in us that's really amazing, but we are the only ones who know. We lie awake and alone in the middle of the night and feel it alive, kicking in us. There often is a unique price to be paid when we are full of the future but it hasn't yet happened. We can only imagine what Mary must have endured during her nine months of pregnancy. Here she is a virginal teenager, pregnant with the future, and ready, if necessary, to lose everything. She almost did.

Fifth, she was willing to give birth. We often talk about the miraculous conception but fail to remember the human element. I'm certain that the birth was laborious, full of travail, as any other birth. In fact, it was probably worse. Stables. Animals. Smells. Dirt floor. Rough hay. Far away from home. Mary was just a young woman giving birth.

I think that too often we miss the balance between something being divinely conceived and what we must do to bring it to life. Baba, for instance, believed that he had a specific calling from God to serve his village. But he had to exercise his will. He had to participate. He had to act.

James taught that "faith by itself, if it is not accompanied by action, is dead" (Jas. 2:17).

History is not already written. Yes, we know how it will all turn out, but we do not know what our own roles in the cosmic drama will be.

—Darrow Miller,
Discipling Nations[2]

We must understand that our actions create history. James Sire wrote, "God created the cosmos as a uniformity of cause and effect in an open system.... God is constantly involved in the unfolding pattern of the ongoing operation of the universe. And so are we as human beings!... If the universe were not orderly, our decisions would have no effect. If the course of events were determined, our decisions would have no significance."[3]

Darrow Miller said, "God has given us the unfathomable privilege of being co-creators with Him. Man, made in God's image, is given the awesome task of bringing forth all the potential of creation... history is open, also; God, angels, and men can intervene to change its course."[4] It's no wonder then that cultures rooted in this ethic believe that life can get better, that progress is possible in the material world. These types of societies not only have hope for the future, but also reflect a sense of ambition, action, discovery, and optimism. They act to make history better.

Though we are predestined, we have the ability to make choices that determine whether or not our destinies will unfold as God has intended. Do not sit around and wait for history to happen to you. While we know the end of the story for the universe, we don't know what our role will be in it. Do not live as if your actions have no impact. Be an actor, not a victim.

An observation about President Ronald Reagan and how his acting skills—of all things—impacted his life story and world history is pertinent here: "The thing about Reagan... is that he was able to make the leap from acting to reality. He understands open-endedness and contingency. He sees that life is a drama in which a lot of the scenes still haven't been written. And recognizing the open-endedness of life makes Reagan a lot more unusual than you might think."[5]

We must have more than a dream. Our grand vision needs to be turned into an actionable plan. We must have the discipline to turn foresight into strategies that we can execute and measure. This is hard work but it must be done: "The future should not be a vague concept and strategy should not be a monstrous task in which we take pride in complexity. Strategy can be simple. Yes, it must be comprehensive, but it doesn't have to be complicated."[6]

Strategic planning begins with strategic thinking. Strategic thinking has to do with "developing insight about the present and foresight about the future."[7] This should be fun, an exercise in creativity. What do you imagine God is saying to you about your future? How does this fit into your present reality? What's going on in the world around you? What is the plethora of paths to seeing your God-inspired future actualize? A good strategic-thinking process studies the environment, educates and tests assumptions, tries to anticipate the future, and begins to articulate imagination.

Our church recently engaged in a six-month strategic-thinking process. We facilitated several creative-thinking sessions with a cross section of church members who have expertise in thinking creatively and/or strategic planning. One of these sessions was led by an executive from a large media firm in the United States. She posed a question about how to accomplish our mission, and then for hours we creatively explored new and better ways for mission fulfillment. We also held a number of focus groups and a lot of informal discussions. That was the fun part. I then took the data, the ideas, and the assumptions about the future that percolated to the surface over those six months and started to organize those thoughts into a strategic plan. That wasn't much fun.

A strategic plan involves a statement of mission, vision, core values, prioritized strategic objectives, goals that are connected to a timeline, and a plan to monitor and measure results. It is an actionable plan. It guides the actions that should be taken in order to achieve specific outcomes in the future.

We must not just talk about the future. We must imagine what it should look like in coming years. What actions should we be taking this year to execute that plan? This month? This week? Today? One of the keys to having purpose and meaning in our lives is to ensure that what we are doing today is connected to our dreams for the future.

Get intentional about your dreams.

Become an expert on your future.

Be creative.

Think.

Organize your thoughts.

Make plans.

Take action.

Chapter 20
Be the Miracle

You must act to make your own history.

Part of my problem in life and leadership is that I want everything to be perfect before I take action. Whether that's trying to master a subject on which I'm about to speak or knowing every detail about some major project, it's hard for me sometimes to just pull the trigger.

Carly Fiorina, former CEO of Hewlett-Packard, wrote about her attempt to bring change to her company's culture:

> So often the instinct was to stand still until every contingency had been prepared for, until every question had been answered, until every possible risk had been defined. Some in Silicon Valley said that the best way to manage a technology company in fast-moving times was described by "Ready. Fire. Aim, aim, aim, aim." By this they meant that fast action and rapid-fire decision making was critical, and once a decision was made, you expended energy to make the decision right. The joke was that the HP management philosophy had become "Ready. Aim, aim, aim, aim..." No one ever fired until absolutely everything was perfect, and so no one ever fired.[1]

Fiorina said she coined the phrase "perfect enough," meaning that at some point, maybe sooner rather than later, you have to decide and execute. Success flows from action. Even something as esoteric as love has to be acted upon to be experienced. Dostoevsky talked about practicing active love. C. S. Lewis called love an act of the will. He said, "Do not waste time bothering whether you 'love' your neighbor; act as if you did. As soon as we do this we find one of the great secrets. When you are behaving as if you loved someone you will presently come to love him."[2] There comes a time when you quit theorizing about love and you start doing love.

I think that this principle applies to a lot of things—love, faith, and our hoped-for dreams. Don't just dream. Practice active dreams. Start to act on what you dream for. Only then will those dreams manifest in your life. We must take action.

The apostle Paul prayed an insightful prayer for the Thessalonians. He prayed that God would "fulfill every good purpose of [theirs] and every act prompted by [their] faith" (1 Thess. 2:11). He assumed that every good purpose of theirs was God-inspired and that the actions they took through faith would be God-blessed.

I think a lot of times our prayers are in response to what's happening to us or around us. But sometimes our prayers need to be about the action we're taking. This is especially true when the action that we're taking has gotten us into a situation where we really need God to work a miracle in order for us to be successful. Don't just pray, "Lord, look at all these things that are happening to me. Help me!" Also pray, "Lord, look at this situation I'm in. I've dreamed big and acted big, and now I really need you to make this thing happen." Create a need gap in your life that is ever widening because you are acting in faith.

Don't pray as a victim; pray as an actor.

Faith takes action. Look at these examples of history makers:

> The act of faith is what distinguished our ancestors, set them above the crowd.... By an act of faith, Abel brought a better sacrifice to God.... By an act of faith, Enoch skipped death.... By faith, Noah built a ship.... By an act of faith, Abraham said yes to God's call.... By an act of faith he lived in the country promised him.... By faith, barren

Sarah was able to become pregnant.... By faith, Abraham... offered Isaac.... By an act of faith, Joseph... prophesied.... By an act of faith, Moses' parents hid him.... By faith, Moses... refused the privileges of the Egyptian royal house.... By an act of faith, Israel walked through the Red Sea.... By faith, the Israelites marched.... By an act of faith, Rahab... welcomed the spies.... I could go on and on, but I've run out of time. There are so many more—Gideon, Barak, Samson, Jephthah, David, Samuel, the prophets.... Through acts of faith, they toppled kingdoms, made justice work, took the promises for themselves. They were protected from lions, fires, and sword thrusts, turned disadvantage to advantage, won battles, routed alien armies.

—Hebrews 11, MSG

The Gospels tell story after story about how people responded to something they wanted from Jesus through active faith. "Do you want more wine? Then fill the jugs with water." "Do you want to get well? Get up!" "Are they hungry? Find them some food." "Do you want to see? Go wash in the pool." "Do you want to be resurrected? Come out of that tomb." (See John 5:6–8; 6:5–6; 9:1–7; 11:38–44.)

Go do something! Get busy. Make the call. Write the check. Schedule the meeting. Do you believe? Act!

In the late 1940s, Samuel Beckett wrote a rather simple two-act play, *Waiting for Godot*. The play consists of only a few characters and a minimal set. The action—or lack of action—is just as uncomplicated. Two hobos, Vladimir and Estragon, are standing idly around, exchanging chit-chat about nothing while waiting for the arrival of "Godot." Every so often, other characters wander onstage and offstage asking what they're doing and the bums repeatedly respond, "We're waiting for Godot."

Nothing much else happens. These two bums continue to aimlessly occupy space for the duration of the play. They argue, make up, engage in small talk, and eat. The simple set changes every scene so the audience can recognize the passing of days. The bums continue to talk and wait, wait and talk, but Godot is a consistent no-show. He never does come. The last few lines of this script are the most quoted and can best demonstrate the life perspective of these bums:

> Vladimir: Well, shall we go?
> Estragon: Yes, let's go.

They do not move.

This play has been interpreted in many different ways; Beckett never stated the specific message he was trying to convey. Some people see it promoting nihilism, the philosophy that life is nothing, void of meaning and purpose. Others believe the play is mocking Christians. I think that's probably true, "nihilistic Christians"—Christians who live as if there is no meaning or purpose in their lives other than to wait.

Some believers are just waiting for Jesus to come. He will. But we must be doing more than just waiting. Others are waiting for their ship to come in, waiting for retirement, waiting to win the lottery, waiting for their big break. They act like those bums, standing around doing nothing while hours pass into days, days pass into months, and months pass into years. Life is happening all around them, but they are not happening to life.

There is a time to wait. Isaiah said, "But those who trust in the Lord will find new strength. They will soar high on wings like eagles. They will run and not grow weary. They will walk and not faint" (Isa. 40:31, NLT). We wait to gain strength to walk, run, fly. We wait on God to figure out what we are supposed to do. We wait because we want our strength to be renewed. We wait, but at some point God shows up, tells us what to do, and then empowers us to start doing it!

Thus, and not otherwise, the world was made. Either something or nothing must depend on individual choices. And if something, who could set bounds to it?

—C. S. Lewis,
Perelandra[3]

Perelandra is the second book of C. S. Lewis's *Space Trilogy*. The leading characters, Ransom and Lady, are the Adam and Eve of the planet Perelandra. They have been placed on this Edenic planet by Maleldil— God. They must battle an evil that has invaded His perfect world. The Un-man, Satan, tirelessly pursues Ransom and the Lady, trying to defeat them, destroy the planet, and create a new and evil world order.

As the battle for Perelandra reaches its climax, Ransom and the Lady are overwhelmed by the awesome role they have been chosen to play: "If the issue lay in Maleldil's hands, Ransom and the Lady were those hands. The fate of a world really depended on how they behaved in the next few hours. The thing was irreducibly, nakedly real. They could, if they chose, decline to save the innocence of this new race, and, if they declined, its innocence would not be saved."[4]

Ransom prays desperately for a miracle, and then he is inspired by God with this penetrating truth—"He himself was the miracle."[5] Ransom, of course, felt like all of us when we realize that we are central to the answer of our own prayers:

> "Oh, but this is nonsense," said the voluble self. He, Ransom, with his ridiculous piebald body and his ten-times defeated arguments— what sort of a miracle was that? His mind darted hopefully down

a side-alley that seemed to promise escape. Very well then. He *had* been brought here miraculously. He was in God's hands. As long as he did his best—and he *had* done his best—God would see to the final issue.[6]

I'm sure you get the point. I've pounded it over and over.

You are the miracle. God wants to use you to do His work. You can make history. You can create the future. So stop sitting there. It's time to take action to make your world and God's world more like what He planned it to be.

Part Five
Reflection Questions

1. James wrote, "Faith without actions is dead." What are some areas in your life where you need to add action to your faith in order to bring life?

2. What does it mean to "sit around and wait for history to happen to you"? What would it look like for you to make history?

3. Consider what it means to pray as an actor rather than a victim. Paul prayed in 2 Thessalonians 1:11 that "God would fulfill...every act prompted by your faith." Write a prayer that has you praying as an actor who is taking action by your faith.

4. What does it mean to "create a need gap in your life that is ever widening because you are acting in faith"?

Part Six

LEAD

Chapter 21
The Obligation of Leadership

THIS IS NOT A self-help book. Who wants to enter into a preferred future alone? That's why the next chapters are about leadership. A moral future is an inclusive one. I want my future to be experienced in the company of many people I've inspired to their own preferred futures.

Leadership is about accepting responsibility for others. We are obligated to more than just ourselves. We are obligated to countless people we have direct or indirect, immediate or future influence over. If we are moral people, we cannot *not* be leaders.

I'm thinking about Charles Valentine. Charles's birth was the byproduct of a sexual assault; his mother chose to marry her rapist. From the beginning, Charles's life was a mess. His family had a long-winded history of multiple suicides, alcoholism, sexual abuse, and insanity. As he grew older, Charles found an escape through money and began making lots of it. At one point, he owned and operated five successful businesses. But being haunted by a legitimate fear of going insane hurled him into a thirty-six-year abusive relationship with drugs and alcohol that got him thrown in jail many times.

So one day he was a successful entrepreneur in the process of acquiring fifteen-plus new businesses, and thirty-some years later—after snorting perhaps millions of dollars' worth of cocaine—he was living in an old Ford Pinto with his dog. He had lost everything and was convinced he would end up sharing the fate of several of his relatives—living in a mental institution—dying from insanity.

Through a series of miraculous events, Charles began the long, arduous journey into recovery. After undergoing treatment in a drug and alcohol rehabilitation center, Charles found his way into our church. He didn't have a car or a driver's license. He did have a criminal record. I was amazed to see Charles, on many occasions, attend every offered weekend service in his desperate want for these preferred-future concepts to penetrate his mind and heart. His life began to transform. Prodigious visions began to be conceived when he realized God had more in store for him—even more than recovery—which was miraculous in itself.

He was tasked with creating our PATH Ministry (Peace over Addiction Through Healing), which meets weekly around the Twelve Steps for Christians and provides a number of programs and services to recovering addicts and alcoholics. Well over a thousand people have gone through this recovery program in the past eight years. Charles is now widely recognized in the metropolitan area as a significant leader in the field of substance abuse recovery.

Four years ago—and seven years into his recovery—Charles married his beautiful wife, Lisa. They have recently founded the Valentine Foundation and have seen their vision to open Valentine Homes, live-in residences for recovering addicts, come true. And thousands of people have been impacted by Charles's book, *The Man in the Tombs*.

By God's grace, Charles has a wonderful life. But it was not enough for him to have a preferred future just for Charles. He is making certain that many others can make the choice to live a wonderful life as well.

Throughout redemptive history, whenever something significant needed to be carried out, God raised up a leader to get it done. The Bible is a collection of stories about men and women chosen by God to influence groups of people toward realizing and actualizing His purposes.

I like the discussion about succession that Moses had with God when he was about to die. He had led Israel to the borders of their preferred future, but he knew that God's dreams for His people would not be accomplished if they didn't have a leader.

So Moses implored God, "May the LORD, the God of every human spirit, appoint someone over this community to go out and come in before them, one who will lead them out and bring them in, so the LORD's people will not be like sheep without a shepherd." So the Lord said to Moses, "Take Joshua...a man in whom is the spirit of leadership, and lay your hand on him" (Num. 27:15–18, NLT).

The New Testament also offers clear and direct appreciation of good leadership: "Remember your leaders, who spoke the word of God to you. Consider the outcome of their way of life and imitate their faith....Have confidence in your leaders and submit to their authority, because they keep watch over you as those who must give an account" (Heb. 13:7, 17, NLT).

Alright, you may say, so our world needs leaders. My assumption is that many of you reading this book already know this. It's generally understood, however, that some 90 percent of us do not see *ourselves* as leaders.

I believe everyone is a leader somewhere. If you are a mother, you are a leader. If you are a teacher, you are a leader. If you are gifted in the arts, you are a leader. Excellent athlete? Leader. Manager? Pastor? Politician? Neurologist? CEO? Obviously, a leader.

There is this infernal question about whether leaders are born or made. I think the answer is yes—leaders are born and made. Richard Daft, in his highly acclaimed text on leadership, wrote that "the diversity of traits that effective leaders possess indicates that leadership ability is not necessarily a genetic endowment....It is important to remember that most people are not born with natural leadership skills and qualities, but leadership can be learned and developed."[1]

Best-selling authors James Kouzes and Barry Posner put it like this: "We've gathered a huge amount of data—from more than 4,000 cases and 200,000 surveys—showing that leadership is an observable, learnable set of practices. After assessing all of this information, the conclusion we've come to is this: Leadership is everyone's business.... Everyone must function as a leader at some time."[2]

Leadership is art and science. It can be studied. Its principles can be observed, learned, and tested. But the artistry of leadership can only be experienced as one accepts the responsibility of leadership and starts leading. Someone can have a God-given inclination for music, for example, but they still must study its science and practice in order to artfully perform. Conversely, someone may not be born with a genetic bent toward music, yet they can still learn to play—although they will have to work harder in order for their performance to be considered artful.

As it concerns leadership, there are those who are born with a proclivity for leadership, or with what we typically consider to be natural leadership traits. Those born leaders still must study how to lead. They must practice leadership in order to learn to lead well. Moreover, it's just as true that someone with an unlikely leadership makeup can, too, study leadership, practice its techniques, and learn to lead well. Leading may be harder for that person, and their leadership may not always appear natural and fluid. But that's okay. Sometimes you just have to go ahead and lead.

God gives us particular gifts for particular purposes: "We have different gifts, according to the grace given to each of us. If your gift is prophesying, then prophesy in accordance with your faith; if it is serving, then serve; if it is teaching, then teach; if it is to encourage, then give encouragement; if it is giving, then give generously; if it is to lead, do it diligently; if it is to show mercy, do it cheerfully" (Rom. 12:6–8, NLT).

God-gifts provide the basis for what we refer to as natural abilities or inborn personal traits. I do not think, though, that any one gift does or should operate exclusively from the others. From testing and experience, I am aware that my strongest gift is leadership. I have also become aware, however, that a leadership gift is nearly worthless, if not dangerous, without the development of other less obvious gifts.

Many people who are gifted with leadership are not inclined "to show mercy." Leaders want to get things done. They want them done now. They typically have little patience for anything or anyone who impedes their progress. I learned many years ago, however, that a pastor with a leadership gift will not be successful if he does not develop his mercy gift.

Most congregations will not follow a person long if he or she has a strong leadership gift with no mercy. Merciless leaders are destined for disaster. After all, if we are Christ followers, how can we not have mercy? His passionate plea for leaders to shepherd people came from His desire to show mercy (Mark 6:34).

Most of you are probably saying "Amen" to this, particularly if you have ever tried to follow a leader with an underdeveloped mercy gift. But why is it that the same "develop-your-other-gifts" standard is not applied to those who have a strong mercy gift but are weak in leadership? People will say they want to be like Jesus. Jesus was not only merciful, Jesus was a leader.

Think about this: A person motivated by mercy wants to start a soup kitchen. But she says things like, "I'm not a leader" or "I don't think I can do that." And then she sits around for years wanting "to show mercy" but never finding a way to show that mercy because she "isn't a leader." Why do we give her a pass? She is obligated to develop the leadership

skills necessary to do what mercy is calling her to. She must learn to lead.
Futures are at stake!

Irish rock star Bono, lead singer of U2, leverages his art and fame
through leadership to rally powerful individuals, churches, and govern-
ments toward radical involvement in addressing the AIDS pandemic:
"It was like, what else are you going to do with this thing called celebrity?...Celebrity is currency—I'm going to spend mine...I am not
Mother Teresa, I'm a rock star...but I have a head for the world's poor. I
am strategic."[3]

What if every one of us took whatever gifts we have and leveraged them
by leading toward some better, best, and preferred end? What kind of
difference would this make in our world?

How often have I heard someone in a place of influence or a leadership
position with a title like doctor, parent, or manager attempt to explain
away some neglect or even gross negligence in leadership by saying, "That's
not my gift?" I fear that this is often used as a cop-out. Leading may not
come naturally to all of us, but we can develop our lesser gifts. We can
learn how to lead.

In the movie *Cinderella Man*, based on a true story, Russell Crowe
starred as Jim Braddock, a promising and talented prizefighter known for
his fierce and even deadly right hand. He was prematurely driven into
retirement after he broke his right hand and suffered a string of losses.
Braddock and his family violently tumbled into bad times and hard luck
during the Great Depression. Day after day, he sought work as a laborer
at the docks three miles away from his home. Forced to operate heavy
machinery and perform hours of heavy lifting with a bum right hand, he

started depending on his left hand out of sheer necessity. It was a matter of survival for his family.

Years later, Braddock was given a golden opportunity to reenter the ring. He fought with stunning precision and an unexpectedly potent force—a devastating left hand. Braddock won that first fight. He went on to win the heavyweight title in 1934 in one of the greatest boxing upsets ever. This world champion wasn't born with a strong left hand; he developed it.

I believe that whether we're born with a leadership gift or not, we can develop it when forced to. Max De Pree wisely suggested, "One becomes a leader, I believe, through doing the work of a leader."[4]

Part of learning by leading occurs through what have been called "adult learning moments."[5] Here's an illustration. You decide to skydive out of an airplane for the very first time. You receive instructions on the ground and listen intently. Then, as the plane is flying 2,500 feet in the air, the instructor yells out final instructions over the roar of the engines. You listen obsessively; there is no way you're going to miss a word of what's being said. You realize how high the stakes are as you prepare to jump. This is an adult learning moment.

Leadership creates constant moments like this. You simply have to learn for your own survival and the survival and success of those you are leading. Trust me; you can learn to lead if you have to! And I think you have to.

Chapter 22
A Place Called Willingness

Young men have strong passions... They would always rather do noble deeds than useful ones... They think they know everything, and are always quite sure about it; this, in fact, is why they overdo everything... Old men have lived many years. They often have been taken in... The result is that they are sure about nothing and under-do everything. They 'think' but they never 'know'... they always add 'possibly' or a 'perhaps'... They lack confidence in the future for most things go wrong, or anyway worse than one expects.

—Aristotle,
Rhetoric

RELUCTANCE AND AMBITION ARE at opposite ends of the "just lead something already" spectrum. Both extremes are dangerous to us and to others. Safety, action, and meaningful accomplishments are found in the vast space between reluctance and ambition. This is a place called willingness.

Generally, there are two kinds of what I call reluctant—"should be"—leaders, those who say "I can't" and those who say "I won't." The "I-can't" person is full of self-doubt and paralyzing insecurities. He may see the need and opportunity for leadership but he timidly responds, "I can't." While that person is well-intentioned and humble, he lacks, in his own mind, the ability to lead.

The "I-won't" person is outright selfish. He sees a need yet refuses to meet it. Often he is aware of the high cost of responsible leadership and so, when challenged to lead, simply answers, "I won't." If most people had this attitude, what kind of families, businesses, churches, and world would we have?

Dramatically juxtaposed with reluctance is ambition. I relate better to this. I must confess that I was born ambitious. This is, perhaps, both my greatest strength and biggest weakness. It wasn't until recent years that I could even begin to understand reluctant leaders. Who wouldn't want to lead? Why would anyone reject an opportunity to make a difference? Ambition, however, is almost always mentioned in the pejorative.

Peggy Noonan writes it this way: "Ambition is a funny word in modern life. It comes with a disapproving sniff—*he's so ambitious*. But no one great became great without ambition; it's a must, a crucial component."

I understand why people sniff at those they consider ambitious. History is littered with stories of those who were ambitious for the wrong things for the wrong reasons. Most of us, through some personal and probably painful experience, know the havoc a driven but improperly motivated leader can wreak.

How do I make sure that my passion to lead, to make a difference, and to create futures is not just dangerous ambition or ego need? Conversely, how does the reluctant leader ensure that their lack of motivation isn't a dereliction of duty? I believe that both of us need to move toward a place called willingness.

Reluctant leaders move to willingness by changing "I can't" and "I won't" into "I am willing." Ambitious leaders move to willingness by changing "I have to lead something" into "I am willing only to accept the opportunities and responsibilities God has planned for me." Vaclav Havel, former president of the Czech Republic, proposed that "the real test of a man is not how well he plays the role he has invented for himself, but how well he plays the role that destiny assigned to him."[1]

I love James and John, the two guys Jesus called "sons of thunder." Why sons of thunder? As young men they were driven to appear successful. They bombastically articulated their desires in a way that has come to personify unsanctified ambition. "'Teacher,' they said, 'we want you to do for us whatever we ask.' 'What do you want me to do for you?' he asked. They replied, 'Let one of us sit at your right and the other at your left in your glory.'"

Wow! Talk about negative audaciousness! James and John wanted to use their access to the Son of God to guarantee their eternal place. They said, "We want to be great and we want everyone to know it forever!" These two Christ-followers seemed opportunistic in the worst sort of way. They were reviled for this brazenness by their peers.

Jesus didn't rebuke their ambition, though. He redirected it: "'You don't know what you are asking,' Jesus said." After all, Jesus had purposely hand-picked these young guys, knowing full well how ambitious they were. He intended to use them to change the world forever. He wanted them to be great, just not in the way they imagined.

Jesus asked them a pregnant question: "Can you drink the cup I drink or be baptized with the baptism I am baptized with?"

"'We can,' they answered." He was asking them if they were willing to suffer with Him, for Him, and for others. He then taught them that leadership was not about title, notability, or the exercise of power: "'You know that those who are regarded as rulers of the Gentiles lord it over them, and their high officials exercise authority over them. Not so with you. Instead, whoever wants to become great among you must be your servant, and whoever wants to be first must be slave of all.'" (See Mark 10:35–44, TNIV.) With this statement, Jesus revolutionized the greatness paradigm.

James and John did become two of the greatest figures in history. James is called James the Great. What was so great about James the Great? He was the first apostle to be martyred in the Christian church.

John is known in history as John the Beloved. He is famous for his relationship to Jesus, his love for the church, and the prophetic insights of his Revelation. In his letters to the church, he explained love and God, as in "God is love" (1 John 4:8), in a way that truly changed the world. John suffered greatly, yet ministered with powerful joy.

James and John moved from ambition to willingness. They changed "we want" to "we will do whatever you ask us to do." In giving themselves to God, His church, and His world, they radically redefined leadership and greatness for us all.

On a more earthly note, I remember the beginning of West Orange mayor Rob Parisi's political career. Fifteen years or so ago, some neighbors joined together to organize the Eagle Rock Civic Association here in West Orange. I happened to be at one of the very first meetings of the association because they were debating whether or not to support an application our church had made to the township's zoning board. One of the main items on their agenda was to elect a president for the organization.

Over the course of an hour or two, several people were nominated, but for some reason or other, every one of them declined the nomination. While all in attendance agreed that having a civic association was a great idea, no one wanted to step up and lead. That is, until Rob, who was not all that well-known in the community at that time, stood to his feet and announced his willingness to serve. In a few minutes, he'd been elected president of the Eagle Rock Civic Association.

Rob did such a great job leading that organization that a few years later he was elected to the West Orange town council, where he served for ten years.

In 2010, he was elected mayor of West Orange.

All of this began because he stood up one day and said, "I accept the responsibility to lead." He was willing. He wanted in.

In my late teenage years, I somehow knew that my calling was to lead a great church in a suburb of New York City. I had never even been to New York City; I just knew that this was my destiny. But youthful immaturity, mixed with this God-calling, produced an overabundance of unrefined ambition.

People would ask me what I planned to do with my life, and I would boldly announce that I was going to lead a church in a suburb of New York City. I would then specify the number of people that I expected to lead. It was an incredibly large number; I'm embarrassed when I think back about it. I started a file detailing the core values of this church, how it would be organized, and some of the big things I believed we would accomplish.

In my early twenties, I experienced a period of personal brokenness as I served on the staff of a local church and traveled to speak in churches around the nation. One day, as I was desperately praying in my darkened office, I had an epiphany of sorts. I was suddenly and acutely aware that my motives for this suburb-of-New-York-City thing were, at best, mixed. There was arrogance in the way I described what I believed about God's plan for my future. Convicted, I got up, turned on the light, opened a drawer in my desk, and pulled out my "dream church" file. I threw it away.

I promised God that I would no longer make this claim of what I'm going to do and where and when and with how many—not until some of that I-want-to-be-great stuff got worked out in my heart. When people would ask me about my plans for the future, I would respond something like this: "You know, I'm really not sure. For right now I just want to be faithful at doing what I'm doing. I know God has great dreams for me, but I'm trying to be careful and to listen and learn better what He's thinking. And I'm really trying to make sure that I want to do the right things for the right reasons."

Through an amazing journey of divine appointments, I was eventually offered the pastorate of a small congregation in a suburb of New York City. When this happened, I was in a different place than I had been just a few years earlier. The pendulum had swung from ambition to reluctance. But it had finally settled in a place called willingness. I only wanted to accept this leadership challenge if this was what God had dreamed for my life.

Kierkegaard submitted that "the thing is to understand myself, to see what God really wishes me to do...to find the idea for which I can live and die."[2] I knew and I know that I had found that idea. Whether you are inclined toward ambition or reluctance, I dare you to say, "Okay, I'll do it. I will accept the responsibility to lead, and I will learn how to lead well." What kind of futures can you lead others to if you'll just be willing?

Perhaps one day you can feel the inevitable joy that accompanies accepting the responsibility to lead others in your area of destiny. Like Paul, who wrote to people whose lives he had influenced in Thessalonica: "For what is our hope...when He comes? Is it not you? Indeed, you are our glory and joy" (1 Thess, 2:19–20, TNIV). Like John, who penned, "I have no greater joy than to hear that my children are walking in the truth" (3 John 1:4, TNIV).

I hope all of us can know that kind of joy. Maybe it means leading a group of teenagers in your local church, inspiring your employees to turn around a struggling business, motivating your team to greater success, or impacting the lives of the third graders you teach. See, it's not enough to come into your own preferred future. You can lead others—lots of others—to a better place as well!

Chapter 23
What Leaders Do

PARDON THE DRAMA...but it was a large moment for our family that January when Sharon and I sat with our eighteen-year-old son Caleb in the office of head football coach Jack Siedlecki at Yale University. We were surrounded by mementos of a rich football tradition in one of the world's great institutions of higher learning. The 2006 Ivy League Championship trophy was strategically placed within our line of sight. More importantly, for me and Sharon, Caleb's future was clearly in sight.

"So, Caleb, do you want to be a Yale Bulldog?" asked Coach Siedlecki. Almost immediately, Caleb replied, "Yes, sir, I do." As I have reflected on the impact this opportunity would have on his future and on the futures of those Caleb will lead, I'm aware that many wonderful people helped prepare him for this favorable time: His mother, who homeschooled him until he was a high school freshman. Marvelous children and youth ministry leaders in our local church. Great teachers at West Orange High School. A myriad of athletic coaches over the years. But concerning the football thing, he had had only one coach: John Jacobs, head football coach at West Orange High School.

Caleb had played baseball since T-ball and was the only sophomore to make the varsity team, earning a 3–0 record as a pitcher that year. He loved basketball and was recognized for his efforts with a number of awards, like a couple of all-conference commendations. But football? He didn't even play football until his junior year. Coach Jacobs saw something special in him and dogged him constantly until Caleb finally decided to give it a try. He started both ways at tight end and defensive end that first year. His team had a terrible season, going 0–10.

Yet Caleb decided not to play baseball his junior year and focused his attention instead on getting ready for football the next season. Somehow, even in the midst of a demoralizing season, Coach Jacobs inspired kids to want to play, to practice hard, and to keep believing—in spite of the fact that a lot of people wondered if West Orange would ever win another football game.

Well, in Caleb's senior season, the Mountaineers went 8–3 and won the first football playoff game in West Orange High School history. Caleb, a team captain, was recognized with many impressive awards and accolades. Most importantly, universities like Yale got interested in a great student with deep character and a sincere faith who could play tight end at a Division I-AA level.

None of this would have happened except for a leader. Coach Jacobs, a retired marine, big, tough and—I'm sure to about any high school kid—pretty intimidating, somehow embodies many of the leadership characteristics you'll read about in this chapter. Young men want to follow him. They sacrifice, in spite of immediate outcomes, to get better. They strive to be team leaders. They know that Coach Jacobs, even with his in-your-face speeches where he's challenging their manhood, deeply loves each of them and is heavily invested in their individual success. He led them from the worst season in their high school's football history to a season that all of them will remember for the rest of their lives.

So what exactly is leadership? Many have diligently dissected this complex topic. Academic analysis locates well over 850 definitions of leadership.[1] I once heard someone remark that the most valuable aspect of art is that which cannot be explained. I think the same is true of leadership.

The greatest qualities of leadership are those which cannot be analyzed or described.

Still, while I recognize the enormity of this subject, I believe there are specific and essential leadership characteristics which, if understood, can help anyone lead more effectively. Here is my definition of moral leadership:

> *Moral leadership is to inspire, influence, and empower people to self-actualization and the accomplishment of mission.*

I want to spend the next two chapters briefly unpacking each aspect of moral leadership as I understand it. Inspire. Influence. Empower. Self-actualization. Accomplishment of mission.

Inspire

Leadership begins from the premise that you want people to follow you because they *want* to follow you—not because they *have* to follow you. If a leader can stimulate the want-to in a follower—the desire to follow the leader to create a preferred future—then that leader is well on his or her way to moral leadership. Good leaders inspire followers.

Frances Hesselbein says that she has a tattoo on her shoulder. It's a leadership-defining truth Peter Drucker taught her: *Leaders of the past tell. Leaders of the future ask.* She's kidding about the tattoo. She's serious about the defining truth.

Inspirational leaders paint a picture of preferred futures. They constantly remind people what's at stake. Any nonprofit that is organized around higher purposes gives leaders an extraordinary platform for inspiration: "In other organizations the person who has position has incredible leverage. In the military, leaders can use rank and, if all else fails, throw people into the brig. In business, bosses have tremendous leverage in the form of salary, benefits, and perks... But in voluntary organizations, such as churches, the only thing that works is leadership in its purest form."[2] Leaders in the for-profit world or any other leadership effort should similarly view inspiration as a fundamental tool.

Every wise leader, whether a manager, a military officer, or a mother—regardless of the power of their position—should consider how to lead those that follow them as if inspiration were their only leadership leverage. This is not to say that other available motivational tools should be abandoned. By virtue of position, some leaders can and should offer rewards and exact consequences. But you—whatever your level of authority—must begin with the conviction that you want people to follow you because they love following you.

Good leaders inspire people. They breathe life into individuals and groups. They animate organizations. They breed the contagion of enthusiasm. They excite people to dream the dreams, take the risks, and make the sacrifices that are necessary to create better futures.

A people unused to restraint must be led, they will not be drove.

—George Washington[3]

George Washington's leadership over the Continental Army in the American War of Independence is a breathtaking illustration of inspirational leadership. Perhaps his supreme challenge was that, in a way unique in history, he was leading people who were free.

Colonel Joseph Reed, one of Washington's military aides, wrote a letter to his wife describing the leadership obstacles Washington faced: "To attempt to introduce discipline and subordination into a new army must always be a work of much difficulty, but where the principles of democracy so universally prevail, where so great an equality and so thorough a leveling spirit predominates, either no discipline can be established, or he who attempts it must become odious and detestable, a position which no one will choose."[4]

There was a critical juncture in the Revolutionary War when many of General Washington's soldiers were overwhelmed by a spirit of defeat. As the hope of independence and the daunting reality of war collided, many soldiers refused to reenlist when their enlistment periods ended. Consequently, these discouraged troops abruptly began to abandon their posts in droves.

In retrospect, this was clearly a pivotal moment in the history of the world. The fate of several billion futures rested on the exhausted shoulders of George Washington and his motley crew of soldiers. So what did he do? He inspired his troops with a speech:

> "My brave fellows, you have done all I asked you to do, and more than could be reasonably expected, but your country is at stake, your wives, your houses, and all that you hold dear. You have worn yourselves out with fatigue and hardships, but we know not how to spare you. If you will consent to stay one month longer, you will render that service to the cause of liberty, and to your country, which you can probably never do under any other circumstances."[5]

And one by one, his men started to step forward, united by the call to freedom and a purpose for which to give even their very lives. In *1776*, David McCullough wrapped up his thoughts about this famed leader's abilities by concluding, "It was Washington who held the army together and gave it 'spirit' through the most desperate of times...above all, Washington never forgot what was at stake and he never gave up."[6]

This is leadership! Leaders can't drive people; they must lead them. How do you lead a daughter in college who can legally make her own decisions? Or an employee who is smarter than you in his area of expertise? Or a potential donor who will share her resources only when and where she is moved to? As Jim Collins wrote, "True leadership only exists if people follow when they have the freedom not to."

> If you can only cajole, not force, if you can only lead, not push, then you make different choices. You can't say, 'Get more excited and insightful or you're fired.' Actually, you can, but it won't work.
>
> —Seth Godin,
> *Linchpin*[7]

How do you motivate free people? How do you "arouse enthusiasm and persistence to pursue a certain course of action"?[8] We must learn to appeal to people's "higher needs." Extrinsic rewards appeal to the lower needs of individuals, such as material comfort, basic safety, and security. Intrinsic rewards appeal to higher needs. Higher needs have to do with a person's need for accomplishment, competence, fulfillment, and self-determination.[9]

People are often motivated to satisfy the fulfillment of their higher needs in a way that actually denies their lower needs. Studies show that how much someone gets paid, for instance, is not the highest motivator. Not that salary level isn't important. It's just not as important as is commonly assumed. Many people will work for lower pay if they have a sense that what they are doing has higher meaning.

Psychologist Frederick Herzberg, one of the great original thinkers in management and motivational philosophy, formed the Two-Factor

Theory. He differentiated between "hygiene factors" and "motivators." Hygiene factors, in an organizational context, relate to basic conditions such as pay, security, company policies, the quality of one's supervisors, and interpersonal work relationships. Herzberg contended that an individual's ultimate job satisfaction does not stem from hygiene factors.

Job satisfaction, rather, flows from what Herzberg identified as motivators. Motivators include people's need for achievement, recognition, a sense of responsibility, finding pleasure in work, and personal growth. Herzberg concluded that though people will express dissatisfaction on the basis of unmet hygiene needs, they will only reveal great fulfillment on the basis of motivators.

Good leaders care deeply about hygiene factors and their followers' lower needs. But leaders understand that most people do not find deep gratification because they are well paid, have a corner office, or have long-term job security. People are content, yet motivated, when their intrinsic needs—their higher needs—are met.

People want meaning.

People want purpose.

People want significance.

If a leader can touch those parts of a person, they can inspire them to give up lesser life for greater life. Jesus taught that sometimes we have to give up our lives to gain that which is truly life (Matt. 16:35). Every organization must find a way to connect each person to higher stuff.

It has been well said that the easiest leadership task is to lead those clearly defined as followers, or to "lead down." But it's a much greater challenge to lead one's peers, or even more so to "lead up." If you have a vision for a preferred future, you will usually have to motivate people who may not be strictly defined as followers, but who still need to follow you.

How does a CEO lead a board of directors? How does a nonprofit leader secure large vision funding from a wealthy donor? How does a team captain motivate other team members? You have to learn how to inspire leaders. You have to be able to articulate preferred futures and remind even other leaders what's at stake.

In *The Talisman*, Sir Walter Scott wrote how Richard the Lionhearted motivated his peers during the Third Crusade. As King of England, Richard was acknowledged as the leader by the other sovereigns who had joined him in this crusade. He became the first among equals—other leaders like the duke of Austria and Philip of France—because of his ability to inspire them and their followers.

Here is a great example: Far from home and having suffered significant military losses, Richard fell gravely ill. His royal brethren were, to a man, weary of war, demoralized by setbacks, and discouraged by the news of challenges in their distant kingdoms. They opportunistically used Richard's weakened state to convene a meeting in his absence. They intended to call off the crusade and lead their armies home. Richard, miraculously delivered from his deathbed, stormed into this meeting and forcibly charged them to honor their pledge to reclaim Jerusalem. The following excerpt from Scott is a little long, but worth it. Look how this guy, Richard the Lionhearted, inspired his peers:

> "But it shames me to remind you of what all but myself seem to have forgotten. Let us rather look forward to our future measures...Or if ye are yourselves a-weary of this war, and feel your armour chafe your tender bodies, leave but with Richard some ten or fifteen thousand of your soldiers to work out the accomplishment of your vow; and when Zion is won," he exclaimed, waving his hand aloft, as if displaying the standard of the Cross over Jerusalem, "when Zion is won, we will write upon her gates, NOT the name of Richard Plantagenet, but of those generous princes who entrusted him with the means of conquest!"

The rough eloquence and determined expression of the military monarch at once roused the drooping spirits of the Crusaders, reanimated their devotion, and, fixing their attention on the principal object of the expedition, made most of them who were present blush for having been moved by such petty subjects of complaint as had before engrossed them. Eye caught fire from eye, voice lent courage to voice. They resumed, as with one accord, the war-cry...and shouted aloud, "Lead us on, gallant Lion's- heart; none so worthy to lead where brave men follow. Lead us on—to Jerusalem—to Jerusalem! It is the will of God—it is the will of God!...

The shout, so suddenly and generally raised, was heard beyond the ring of sentinels who guarded the pavilion of Council, and spread among the soldiers of the host, who, inactive and dispirited by disease and climate, had begun, like their leaders, to droop in resolution; but the reappearance of Richard in renewed vigour, and the well-known shout which echoed from the assembly of the princes, at once rekindled their enthusiasm, and thousands and tens of thousands answered with the same shout of "Zion, Zion!...It is the will of God—it is the will of God!"[10]

How do you lead princes? You begin by inspiring them!

The wisest man who ever lived uttered the wisest words ever offered on this inspiration thing: "Where there is no vision, the people perish" (Prov. 29:18, KJV). The word *vision* here means divine revelation. "Where there is no revelation, the people cast off restraint" (TNIV).

To inspire people to work hard and sacrifice for a great cause, we must have a divine revelation of the future. Then we must learn to communicate that dream. The highest possible inspiration is when people are aware that what they are doing is in line with God-designed purposes and linked to eternal reasons and rewards. They must believe that what they are doing today matters forever. Inspired people will want to follow us to preferred futures.

If there is a spark of genius in the leadership function at all, it must lie
in this transcending ability...to assemble—out of all the variety of
images, signals, forecasts and alternatives—a clearly articulated vision
of the future that is at once simple, easily understood, clearly desirable and energizing.

—Warren Bennis,
Leaders: Strategies for Taking Charge[11]

Influence

Good leaders don't just inspire; they influence. Influence is "the effect
a person's actions have on the attitudes, values, beliefs, or actions of
others...the degree of actual change."[12] Inspiration can be a warm and fuzzy
thing; influence is about outcomes.

This can bring, especially for grand endeavors, no small level of pain.
But real leaders don't just talk about dreams, they make dreams come true.
They turn ideas into reality. They actually create preferred futures.

A leader is not someone who just gets people all fired up with no place
to go. Leaders move people to see a better picture of their lives and their
world and then take action to deliver on possibility. Leaders exact the
discipline necessary to bring transformation. Leadership is not a popu-
larity contest.

It's normal for all of us to want to be liked, and, furthermore, the support
of constituents and the building of consensus are necessary components
of moral leadership. But likeability must be invested in transformation.
What good does it do to be liked if you aren't making a positive difference?

Leaders who are actually committed to change severely threaten the protectors of the status quo. Pulitzer-prize winner Edmund Morris authored a series of fantastic biographies of President Theodore Roosevelt. In his highly acclaimed second work, he wrote that American statesman Elihu Root "warned" an audience of fellow Republicans about the radical influence of this president:

> He is not safe for the men who wish to prosecute selfish schemes for the public's detriment. He is not safe for the men who wish the Government conducted with greater reference to campaign contributions than to the public good. He is not safe for the men who wish to drag the president of the United States into a corner and make whispered arrangements.[13]

President Roosevelt made some fellow politicians visibly uncomfortable by his desire to shake things up to better the nation. A White House correspondent chronicled the apprehension of two Senators he overheard conversing at a dinner party: "It is not so much what he [Roosevelt] had done as what he may do that fills [them] with anxiety... They have been accustomed to a certain way of playing the game. They know the rules... Naturally the question arises in many minds: What of the future? What will it come to?"[14] Good leaders are not safe leaders.

There is a vast difference between transactional leadership and transformational leadership:

> Transactional leadership approaches people on the basis of exchange: making deals, bargaining... by appealing to people's wants or needs. The leader and follower trade for mutual profit, advantage and gratification. As long as the leader is giving a good deal, the follower continues to do business with him; thus the follower's opinion of what the leader does for them becomes more important than what the leader may ultimately accomplish.[15]

This is in stark contrast to transformational leadership, which is "based on change: making a difference rather than a deal, altering people instead of merely appealing to them."[16] You know you are a transformational leader when the people and environment around you are actually changing. Furthermore, if you can survive the initial instinctive resistance to change that comes from most people you will live to be loved more by those same people because you inspired them to better, best, and preferred.

Leaders love people. But this kind of love is so much more than a feeling. They do whatever it takes to help those they lead achieve their highest potential. I like to say that to love is to will the ultimate good for one's self and others. Love and discipline are closely related. The Bible says that if parents love their children, they discipline them (Prov. 3:12). This is not about punishment; it's about training. It's about willing the ultimate good for another. It's about love.

A leader who says he loves people but doesn't challenge them to change is not a good leader. Dr. M. Scott Peck taught that "to fail to confront when confrontation is required for the nurture of spiritual growth represents a failure to love equally as much as does thoughtless criticism or condemnation and other forms of uncaring."[17]

Dr. Peck also promotes what he calls "judicious loving": "Love is not simply giving, it is judicious giving, and judicious withholding as well. It is judicious praising and judicious criticizing. It is judicious arguing, struggling, confronting, urging, pushing, and pulling in addition to comforting. It is leadership."[18]

Chapter 24
What Leaders Do It For

GREAT LEADERS MULTIPLY INSPIRATION and influence by turning their followers into leaders. Leadership professors Charles Manz and Henry Sims called leaders who helped followers learn to lead "superleaders."[1]

Empower

Moral leaders exercise power for good purposes. Essential to this is that they do not hoard power, they give it away: "There is no leadership without power...However, a leader will frequently want to distribute rather than to maintain power."[2] Leaders empower their followers.

One of my greatest learnings as a leader, simple as it is, is that people around me bring gifts, experiences, abilities, and passions in their areas of calling that far surpass what I have to offer. Philippians offers a great leadership lesson when it teaches us to "be humble, thinking of others as better than yourselves" (Phil. 2:3, NLT).

The first key to empower others is to learn to appreciate the gifts that they bring. Max Dupree wisely wrote:

> I happen to believe that a large part of the secret lies in how individual leaders in a great variety of settings make room for people who have unusual gifts and temporarily become followers themselves...a leader first makes a personal commitment to be hospitable to gifted people, a broad commitment to open herself to contributions from many quarters.[3]

The empowerment of others is critical to having high-capacity people journey with you into a preferred future. Empowered people experience self-efficacy: They feel that what they're doing matters. They have ownership of the vision and the ability to exercise power and effect change. They can influence outcomes. Empowered people believe that if they don't show up and dream and think and create, the mission of the organization will not be accomplished.

One of my great joys has been watching some of my team members succeed in their areas of calling in ways that eclipse any success I may have experienced. Years ago I would have felt intimidated by this. This is ridiculous.

Michael Deaver, longtime confidant of Ronald Reagan, described how the president "both attracted and demanded the best people. Nobody threatened him. Some people, regardless of their position are fearful that a subordinate might outshine them. Reagan was just the opposite. He hoped that his subordinates would be smarter than him. If he could bring in a young genius with more muscular IQ so be it."[4]

The second key to empower others is to never fall into the "I'll just do it myself" mindset. Just doing it yourself is not leadership, and this frame of reference is insufferably limiting to one's self and to others. Some of us feel, say, and do this because we have a heightened sense of our own importance or deep insecurities. Others of us don't understand how selfish we are when we don't empower the people who work with us and for us.

Just today, I was doing some consulting with an employer who is a just-do-it-myselfer. She has a young, energetic, intelligent, and talented direct report who is not being asked to do critical work. I stressed how vital it is that this employee be given a serious set of responsibilities, the training and resources necessary to fulfill them, the ability to make decisions concerning them, and the opportunity to succeed or fail as a result. This is not just because the boss needs someone to do a job (which the boss does need), but more so because this employee is not going to be motivated to care about the organization and her role in it if she is not challenged in a consequential way.

Max Depree posited, "Clergy often see delegation as a shirking of their duty rather than a gracious act of involvement. I believe we need to think more carefully about what delegation ought to bring to our own—and others'—career development, to our personal journey, to the need to involve those people with special gifts."[5] I have come to believe that when I refuse to spread responsibility, information, and authority throughout the organization I lead, I commit a destructive act of utter selfishness.

Empowerment is not about a senior leader saying, "I have too much work to do." It's about recognizing that there are too many needs, the cause is too great, and there is too much untapped potential in aspiring leaders. Someone else may actually be able to do what needs to be done better than you. You can't afford to keep all of the inspire-and-influence ability to yourself.

So the first key to empower others is to appreciate the gifts they bring. The second is to expand others and multiply your own leadership power by offering the gift of involvement. *The third key is to learn how to become an effective coach of those you have empowered.*

Empowering others does not in any way mitigate your ultimate responsibility. Rather, in important ways, you must now work harder than ever to ensure that the leaders you are leading have the greatest possibility of leadership success.

You can't empower people, wish them luck, pat them on the back, shove them out the door, and hope they accomplish their goals. As we've discussed, leadership is not "I'll just do it myself," but neither is it saying to those who work with us, "Just do it yourself."

What do great coaches do? Coaches help people become more than they realize they can be...Today's leader is a people developer and relationship builder who asks, "How can I help this person become more valuable as an individual—as well as to all of us?" Today's leader is a coach...A leader leads, much like a coach coaches, to achieve his or her destiny of helping others achieve their destinies.[6]

I think most leaders find it much easier to personally execute than to teach others how to execute. Larry Bird, the former Boston Celtic, was one of the greatest players to ever play the game of basketball. He had an amazing ability to put his team on his shoulders and do whatever needed to be done, especially in the big moments, to win a big game.

When he became coach of the Indiana Pacers, I'm sure it was tortuous at times, especially during the closing seconds of a close game, to only be able to call a time-out, gather his team around him, and draw a play on a white board. But that's what coaches do. They figure out how to help others learn to win.

Coaching is something that must be done up-close and personal. Sometimes it's easier to lead from a distance. It probably does not speak well of me that I relate on some level to Dostoevsky's account of the elder who said:

"I love humanity, but I am always amazed at myself: The more I love humanity in general, the less I love man in particular...I have often made enthusiastic schemes for the service of humanity...and yet I am incapable of living in the same room with anyone for two days together, as I know by my experience. As soon as anyone is near me, his personality bothers me and suffocates my freedom. In twenty-four hours I begin to hate even the best of men; one because he's too long over his dinner; another because he has a cold and keeps on blowing his nose. I become hostile to people the moment they come close to me. But it has always happened that the more I detest men individually the more ardent becomes my love for humanity."[7]

Now, look, I don't hate anybody. I can say, though, it's relatively easy for me to stand up in front of a large crowd and give an inspirational talk that fires everybody up. But somebody I've fired up often becomes a volunteer or a staff team member with whom I end up sitting in a room talking about doing whatever they got fired up to do.

What is this person's idea? How should this project be planned? How should they recruit other volunteers? How are they going to raise funds? How will they negotiate inevitable problems? How will they handle their success? Now I have to coach them. Truth be told, I enjoy inspiring a crowd more than I enjoy coaching individual leaders. But I have to be committed to helping the people I've inspired become successful.

At the same time, I must be careful not to overcoach. I have to remember to give people the freedom to decide, act, make mistakes, and come back strong again. I must not excessively issue directives. I have to take great care to not allow those who work with me to delegate their problems up to me. I must insist that they become problem solvers themselves and leaders in their own right. I want my team members to be more than just an extension of me. I must nurture what they've been inspired to do so that they become better than me in what they have been called to do.

On July 19, 1982, Don Bennett, on one leg, fulfilled a ten-year dream to become the first amputee to climb to the summit of 14,408-foot Mt. Rainier. During a particularly difficult portion of the climb, he had to cross a dangerous ice field—an almost inconceivable task with only one boot with a crampon attached and two crutches: "Unfortunately...Bennett got stuck in the ice. He determined that the only way to get across the ice field was to fall face forward onto the ice, pull himself as far forward as he could, stand up, and then fall forward again. He was going to get across the ice field by falling down."[8]

His teenage daughter, Kathy, who was a part of this expedition, was alongside her father as he labored in this fashion for a ghastly four hours. "She shouted in his ear, "You can do it, Dad. You're the best dad in the world. You can do it!"[9]

Reflecting on the experience, Bennett commented, "There was no way that I was not going to make it across the ice field with my daughter shouting that in my ear. You want to know what leadership is? What she did is leadership."[10] Kathy coached her dad every laboriously painful step of the way. This is what leaders do.

But why? Why do leaders do this? They do it for the self-actualization of others.

Self-Actualization

Leaders serve the dreams of their followers. The story is told about a four-year-old girl who got lost in a big city. As the girl wandered hopelessly, unable to find her way home, she was picked up by a police officer. When he realized that in her fear the girl had forgotten her address, he drove around to see if she could find her home. Finally she cried out, "Wait, there's my church. I can always find my way home from here."[11]

This is what I want people who are a part of the congregation I lead to say: "This is my church, and I can go anywhere from here." When I say *moral leadership is to inspire, influence, and empower people to self-actualization and the accomplishment of mission*, I am highlighting the imperative that leaders must never be only about accomplishing personal or organizational goals. Leaders care deeply about the self-actualization of their followers.

Leaders inspire people to have an ever-expanding vision of all that their lives can be. They make sure that those they influence are always getting bigger inside. I do not believe that a leader has to make a decision between helping people reach their individual potential and accomplishing organizational objectives. Both should and do happen at the same time. If I build big people, they usually bring that bigness into the life of the church in ways that help the church expand its capacity to fulfill its mission. And as the church gets bigger in every way, somehow that bigness stimulates the "what's possible for me" in the hearts of its people. Inexplicably, as people get bigger, the church gets bigger. Conversely, as the church gets bigger, people get bigger. This really excites me!

I remember when Ken Bittman told me that for years he had worked in a large corporation as, in his words, a "computer geek." He said that though he had worked very hard, he had spent most of his time "cowering in his office" avoiding interaction with people and had absolutely no desire to do anything more than perform well in his own job. He said he especially had no desire to lead anything. Then he got outsourced.

Ken found a job as an assistant administrator at a highly regarded nursing home about a year and a half ago. Around this same time, he started attending our church. He told me that it amazed him how often I spoke about leadership in my weekend talks, and he related how, as a result, he made a conscious decision to become a leader. Then he was awarded the position of nursing home administrator, leading a staff of 150 people. I think Ken would say you can find your way anywhere from his church. I hope so. I love to see the people I'm leading succeeding in every area of their lives.

Perhaps the best way to describe this type of leadership is to use the term popularized by Robert Greenleaf—"servant leadership." Greenleaf taught that a servant-leader puts the needs of their followers before their own. The success of an organization is gauged not by what the leader has accomplished, but by whether or not the lives of the individuals in it have been bettered.

Good leadership happens—and it comes in all kinds of packages. There are quiet leaders and bombastic ones. There are analytical leaders and more impulsive ones. Some are tough as nails with their teams, others more nurturing. On the surface, you would be hard-pressed to say what qualities these leaders share. Underneath, you would surely see that the best care passionately about their people—about their growth and success.

—Jack Welch,
Winning[12]

I feel pretty good knowing that the people around me recognize how much I care about their success. But there are other stories, which I'd rather not tell, where I don't come off looking so hot. I'll tell you one.

I had a staff team member come into my office and tender her resignation. I was shocked. This woman assured me that she respected me and believed in what we were doing, but that it was time for her to move on to a new season in her life. I found myself telling her how valuable she was to the organization and what a loss this would be for the rest of the staff team and to me personally. "We need you!" I said. Finally she stopped me and said something simple yet profound. "What about me? What about what I need? What about my future? What do you really know about me and what I want for my life?"

I immediately realized that I had made a classic mistake. I was appealing to her on the basis of the organization's needs—and the leaders' needs. What I somehow had failed to communicate was how much I cared for her and her needs. Moral leaders care deeply about the self-actualization of those they lead.

The person who influences me most is not he who does great deeds but he who makes me feel I can do great deeds.

—Mary Parker Follett,
The New State[13]

The Accomplishment of Mission

Moral leaders are responsible for bringing preferred futures to pass. Inspiring, influencing, and empowering people to self-actualization must ultimately lead to the accomplishment of mission.

Is what you believe God dreamed for your life, your family, your ministry, or your business coming to pass?

When some people talk about what I call moral leadership, I get the idea that the assumption is that as long as we all feel good, it doesn't really matter whether or not the mission gets accomplished. But I don't believe that we were meant to just sit around singing *Kumbaya*. We have been called to do great things.

Jesus Christ couldn't have cared more about those who followed Him, yet He called them to unimaginable sacrifice in fulfilling His mission on this planet. And He still calls us to finish His work. Moral leaders will accept nothing less than seeing come to pass the better future that's in the mind of God for every person in this world. And they are willing to do whatever it takes to get the job done.

Chapter 25
Who Leaders Are

A leader's capacity to make moral choices is related to the individual's level of moral development.

—Richard Daft,
The Leadership Experience

THE MOVIE *THE ALAMO* is based on the epic 1836 San Antonio, Texas, standoff about a group of courageous men who were fighting for the independence of Texas. They were surrounded by the apparently invincible army of Mexican dictator General Santa Anna. In one poignant scene, in the dead of night, Davy Crockett and James Bowie are soberly looking over the wall of the Alamo, gravely aware that in the absence of a miracle, they and everyone else in the fort would die there. A number of their comrades had been quietly escaping into the night, attempting to slip through Santa Anna's lines and on to safety.

Bowie begins to playfully tease Davy about his famous wildcat-skin hat, and Davy sheepishly admits he only started wearing it because of a popular play that had been written about him. Bowie goads him further: "Which was tougher, jumping the Mississippi or riding that lightning bolt?... Can you really catch a cannon ball?" A clearly uncomfortable Davy pauses for a moment and then makes a startling confession: "If it was just me, simple ol' David from Tennessee, I might drop over that wall some night and take my chances—But that Davy Crockett feller... They're all watching him."

Davy Crocket experienced a sentiment common to most leaders at some point. At times, we would, especially at severe stress points, like to be free to act like everyone else—to escape—but the expectations of leadership force us to do the right thing, the honorable thing, the courageous thing. We are bound by the responsibility of leadership. Maybe if it were just us, just our normal human selves, wrestling with temptation, or fear, or weariness, or discouragement, we would just give in or give up or just slip away in the night. But we know we can't.

Our kids are watching us. Or the community we serve. Or the media. Or the stockholders. The fact is, we aren't just "simple ol' David from Tennessee." We are leaders. There is far too much depending on us to ever just run away. We must have the right stuff in us. We must be wired with strong moral fiber. We must live and act virtuously.

Somebody is watching us.

Warren Bennis made the important observation that "leadership always comes down to a question of character."[1] Solomon is known as the wisest man who ever lived and one of history's great leaders. The origin of his wisdom and greatness was in the depth of his character, especially as a young man. There is a famous story about the queen of Sheba, who had "heard of Solomon's reputation, which brought honor to the name of the Lord" and who traveled to Jerusalem to "test him with hard questions" (1 Kings 10:1, NLT):

> When she met with Solomon, they talked about everything she had on her mind. Solomon answered all her questions; nothing was too hard for the king to explain to her. When the queen of Sheba realized how wise Solomon was, and when she saw the palace he had built, she was breathless. She was also amazed at the food on his tables, the organization of his officials and their splendid clothing, the cupbearers and their robes. . . . She exclaimed to the king, "Everything I heard in my country about your achievements and wisdom is true!

I didn't believe it until I arrived here and saw it with my own eyes. Truly I had not heard the half of it! Your wisdom and prosperity are far greater than what I was told. How happy these people must be! What a privilege for your officials to stand here day after day, listening to your wisdom! The LORD your God is great indeed!"

—1 Kings 10:2–9, NLT

At this juncture in Solomon's life, I see him as a supreme example of moral leadership. Here are three reasons: *First, his reputation brought honor to God.* The queen of Sheba was so impressed with him that she was impressed with his God: "Your God is great indeed!" (v. 9).

Second, he served his followers. "How happy and privileged these people are!" (v. 8).

Third, Solomon's achievements were legendary. His accomplishments left the queen breathless and amazed. This is where she famously exclaimed, "Everything I heard about your achievements and wisdom is true!" (v. 6). In fact, "the half has not yet been told" (v. 7).

It is possible for a leader's legacy to be both moral and legendary. I recently traveled to Germany with my son Caleb, along with both of his grandfathers, for Caleb's high school graduation gift. We spent considerable time in the Museum of German History in Berlin. I was struck again by the powerful "leadership skills" of Adolph Hitler and how much he "accomplished" in his short time on the world stage. But because he was immoral and led people to terrible things, his name lives in ignominy. His achievements were legendary...but they exist in infamy because he used immoral means to accomplish evil ends.

At the other extreme, I think about an innocuous leader like, let's say, Jimmy Carter as United States president. It is generally conceded that though President Carter is a good and decent man and, as a former president, has advanced important humanitarian causes, he didn't seem to accomplish much as the most powerful man in the world. Now that's probably an overgeneralization. There were the Camp David Peace Accords, for instance, but my sense is that he was not as effective a leader as one might have hoped. The American electorate invited him to leave office after his first term. President Carter could write a book about being a basically moral person in a position of power, and I would be interested in reading it. But a book on using power and leveraging leadership? I'd pass. See, as a leader, it's not enough to have achieved much, nor is it enough to just be a good person or an all-around nice guy. You need both. Solomon's achievements were legendary and accomplished in a way that honored God and served his followers. That's part of what moral leadership is.

When I think about Solomon's success as a leader, I go back to the understanding that his greatness flowed from the deepest level of who he was. It emanated from his subconscious, from the innermost recesses of his heart. We know this from a seminal experience that Solomon had with God early in his leadership adventure.

One night, as Solomon was asleep, God spoke to him in a dream:

> "'What do you want? Ask, and I will give it to you!' Solomon replied... 'Give me an understanding heart so that I can govern your people well and know the difference between right and wrong.' ... So God replied, 'Because you have asked for wisdom in governing my people... I will give you what you asked for! I will give you a wise and understanding heart such as no one else has ever had or ever will have!'"
>
> —1 Kings 3:5, 9, 11–12, NLT

Solomon made the most critical decision in his life while he was asleep! Out of the depths of his subconscious mind, in a dream, he had the wherewithal to ask God for the ability to discern between right and wrong and for the wisdom he needed to be a good leader. Making the most crucial decisions in my life while I am asleep—in my dreams—is a disturbing thought! The fact is, though, that most of what we are and achieve flows from the subterranean levels of who we are. From the deepest part of our thought and feeling. From our character. This is the source of moral leadership.

Perhaps this is what Solomon meant when he warned us, "Above all else, guard your heart, for everything you do flows from it" (Prov. 4:23, TNIV). The heart is understood to be the most important organ of the human body, and in Scripture the word *heart* "came to stand for man's entire mental and moral activity, both the rational and the emotional elements...it denotes the seat of moral nature and spiritual life...the desires, the affections, the perceptions, the thoughts...the conscience, the intentions...the will."[2] Ultimately what is in our hearts affects absolutely everything that we do. Moral leadership begins in the heart.

Richard Daft writes that there are three levels of personal moral development: pre-conventional, conventional, and post-conventional. Pre-conventional is the most immature stage, typically evidenced in young children or any individual who only keeps the rules because they are afraid of consequences. The conventional level is where someone adopts and follows the moral norm of the culture around them. They do what is expected, not necessarily because of their own deep convictions but because they know it is the correct thing to do.

The post-conventional stage of moral development, or "principled level," is when "leaders are guided by an internalized set of principles universally recognized as right or wrong."[3] Studies show that only about 20 percent of Americans operate at the level of principled development. Principled leaders are the kind of leaders who are going to do what's right regardless of positive or negative consequences or what everyone else is doing. They follow an internal moral code that, at times, causes them to walk against the wind of prevailing culture. They do what is right because of what is in their hearts.

Being fully formed in our moral character is the basis of moral leadership. I am not advocating internal perfection. To do so would make me a hypocrite. I am promoting a constant guarding of the heart—a realization that leadership that creates a better world starts first in the formation of the inner life of the leader. True success always flows from character.

> A leader is a person who has an unusual degree of power to create the conditions under which other people must live and move and have their being—conditions that can either be as illuminating as heaven or as shadowy as hell. A leader is a person who must take special responsibility for what's going on inside him or her self, inside his or her consciousness, lest the act of leadership create more harm than good.
>
> —Parker Palmer,
> *Leading from Within*

Leadership is power. This justifiably frightens a lot of people because power has to do with the ability to act, to assert authority, and to influence others to act and to effect change. Because leadership is about the exercise of power, it is essential that leaders have a basic morality—wisdom and the faculty to discern between right and wrong.

Craig Johnson observed, "We admire powerful leaders who act decisively but can be reluctant to admit that we have and use power. Our refusal to face up to the reality of power can make us more vulnerable to the shadow side of leadership."[4]

Power is dangerous in the hands of the wrong people. Lord Acton did famously say, "Power tends to corrupt; absolute power corrupts absolutely."[5] Power, however—the ability to influence change—can be a wonderful thing if in the hands of the right people with right hearts.

Charles Colson, now one of the most respected moral thinkers and leaders in the world, experienced the unscrupulousness of unfettered power while working in President Nixon's inner circle during the Watergate scandal. He ended up serving seven months in prison as a result. Colson, who became a follower of Jesus Christ while incarcerated, now offers this insight on the use of power: "It is crucial to note that it is power that corrupts, not power that is corrupt. It is like electricity. When properly handled, electricity provides light and energy; when mishandled it destroys... It is the use of power... that is at issue... The temptation to abuse power confronts everyone."[6]

God is not afraid of power; He celebrates it: "For since the creation of the world God's invisible qualities—his eternal power and divine nature—have been clearly seen" (Rom. 1:20). God has ultimate power, but also ultimate character. His power is balanced by His nature.

One of my favorite illustrations on the subject of power tells of a little boy who was admiring a shiny, brand-new sports car parked on a quiet street. He made slow, deliberate circles around the stunning vehicle, admiring its beauty from every angle. As he pressed his nose up against one of the windows to get a better view of the interior, he was startled by a hovering shadow and a booming voice. It was the owner of the four-wheeled beauty.

"What are you doing?" the friendly man asked.

"I'm just looking at this awesome car," the boy replied with a huge grin.

The owner laughed and said, "I'm glad you like my car. You know, my brother gave it to me."

The wide-eyed young lad reflected for a brief moment, and then gave a classic response. "Boy, I sure wish I was a brother like that."

He said what? "I wish *I* was a brother like that?" That wouldn't have been the first instinct many of us would have had. Of course, the little boy in this story got it right. Moral leadership does not mean being in a position of power in order to get, but rather in order to give. We must use power to do good.

Richard Codey has been an influential leader in government in New Jersey for many years. He just finished serving as governor of this state during a time of what many would consider a moral crisis. Governor James McGreevy confessed to an affair with a male appointee in his administration and resigned. Codey, as the Senate majority leader, automatically replaced him.

I've known Codey for a number of years, partly because I have made an effort to have relationships with influencers, but mostly because of my relationship with his dad and Codey's relationship with my boys. His father owned a funeral home in West Orange and went out of his way to be kind to me when I was a new and young pastor in town. Codey's dad, who has since passed away, was a really fine man. My boys are, I humbly offer, outstanding athletes, and Governor Codey, who has an inordinate passion for basketball, has coached each of them over the years on traveling basketball teams.

When Codey ascended to the governorship, I watched the talking heads on national news trying to figure out how he would respond to his new position. Would a new level of power change this fundamentally decent man? Most of us who knew him were already pretty sure that the short answer was no.

Codey always had a passion for mental health issues. He rose to power as a young senator when in the 1980s he went undercover at Marlboro Psychiatric Hospital, posing as a night orderly. During this covert operation, he exposed the degrading, inhumane treatment of mental patients. This legendary undertaking led to numerous reforms that significantly improved the quality of life and care in mental hospitals all over the state. Codey has since constantly fought for positive mental health initiatives. So, on his first day as governor, he had lunch at Greystone Park Psychiatric Hospital and signed an executive order establishing the Governor's Task Force on Mental Health.

On a personal level, he continued to coach my son Christian's basketball team. He had coached these kids for years, and nothing changed when he was governor. On Sunday afternoons, he could be found at Roosevelt Junior High School teaching basketball to a small group of sweaty twelve-year-old boys. On several occasions he picked up Christian to take him to the rare away game that Sharon or I could not attend—two black SUVs and bodyguards with Governor Codey and an adolescent boy sitting in the backseat talking about life and basketball. Not only did Governor Codey use power for good purposes, he continued being the same person he'd always been.

I have no illusions about Dick Codey's imminent sainthood. We are all imperfect human beings. Frankly, I disagree with him frequently about political and social issues. But he models an important part of moral leadership: who we are always shows up. Position and power must not change us. We must guard our hearts and use influence for good purposes.

Moral leadership flows from who we are. Period.

Chapter 26
Who Leaders Are Leading For

MOST OF US WRESTLE with issues of power, character, and morality. I do. I know people are watching me and expect much of me. The ultimate test, though, is what God sees when He looks in me. Can He trust me to lead? Can He trust me with spiritual power? I need to know that when God looks at the essential qualities of my heart that He likes what He sees.

Soren Kierkegaard wrote this about corporate worship: "We suffer from a certain role confusion in worship. Most people imagine that the congregation is the audience, the preacher is a performer, and that God is present as prompter. In fact the congregation are the actors, the preacher is a prompter, and God is the Audience." This principle, of course, not only applies to corporate worship but also to the offering of every part of our lives to God. We live with God as the Audience. This prompts me to ask the question, "If God is the Audience, what kind of Audience is He?"

Is He cheering? Is He disappointed? Is He shouting my name? Does He believe I can win? Is He for me?

For many years, I was terrified when I thought about God really seeing what was going on in me. I used to feel a perpetual wretchedness, a constant awareness of the "woe-is-me-for-I-am-unclean-and-undone" feeling expressed by the prophet Isaiah in God's presence (Isa. 6:5). This recognition of our human weakness before God is, in proper balance, important: "The fear of the Lord is the beginning of knowledge" (Prov. 1:7). But I've also learned that God is able to sort through the good, the bad, and the ugly and to still somehow believe in me and be for me.

I started to see passages like this one in a new light: "The Lord is the One who judges me.... He will bring to light things that are now hidden in darkness, and will make known the secret purposes of people's hearts. *Then God will praise each one of them*" (1 Cor. 4:3–5, NCV, EMPHASIS ADDED). And the magnificent 139th psalm, where David said God had examined his heart and knew everything about him: "You know my thoughts.... You know everything I do...I can never get away from your presence!" (vv. 2, 3, 7, NLT). This thought used to petrify me, but now I see that David perceived this as great news. Why? Because he continued, "How *precious* are your thoughts about me, O God. They cannot be numbered! I can't even count them; they outnumber the grains of sand!" (vv. 17–18, NLT, EMPHASIS ADDED). Yes, God sees everything, but He is looking for the things in us that He can applaud.

God did not have amazing thoughts about David because he was perfect. Far from it. David made some terrible moral decisions, but somehow God was still able to look at David in the whole of his life and feel good about him. I think part of this is that David, when forced to face his issues, didn't try to justify his failings or act as if there was no connection between his private conduct and his public leadership.

- He made mistakes.
- He suffered the consequences.
- He sincerely repented.
- He received God's mercy.
- He was restored.
- He kept leading.

At the end of the day, David was a man after God's own heart who wanted to do God's will, and God liked what he saw (Acts 13:22).

In a famously tender scene at the Last Supper, Jesus looked at his disciples and said, "'You are clean, though not every one of you.' For He knew who was going to betray him [Judas], and that was why He said not every one was clean" (John 13:10–11, TNIV). He called them clean knowing fully that most of them would abandon him in just a few hours. In fact, He told them that they would stumble (Matt. 26:31). He knew Simon Peter was about to deny Him. But Jesus's view of His followers was just the snapshot of their failures surrounding the crucifixion.

He saw the entirety of their lives and the totality of who they were. He knew that although Peter would stumble, his faith wouldn't fail and that someday his stumbling experience would help him strengthen others (Luke 22:31–34). Jesus not only saw the mistakes they would make, He also saw their desire to do good and their future courageousness. He knew that their hearts were to follow Him. He saw the whole picture at the Last Supper, and He was able to find, in each of them, something to believe in.

Now, Judas was another matter. Why? It is one thing to stumble; it's another to betray. Judas willfully and wantonly rebelled and then ran from his mistake into self-destructive oblivion. When Peter came to himself, he wept bitterly, he repented, and he declared his love. Jesus is able to make the distinction between a Judas and those who really have the desire to do the right thing.

Over the years, I have had the opportunity to have spiritual conversations with a lot of people, many of whom question what God thinks of them. They are aware of their own struggles. They are sometimes so disappointed in themselves that they wonder how God could have any good thoughts about them. Most of us are harder on ourselves than God is. Not that He overlooks our shortcomings, but His "kindness leads [us] toward repentance" (Rom. 2:4). His goal is not to condemn us, but to save us. I have seldom met a Judas, but I've met a lot of people who stumble and whom I believe Jesus looks at in the whole of their lives and says, "You are clean."

The reason that this is so important to me is that I believe having confidence to approach God is essential for Him to fix what's broken within us. We need God actively working in our lives. We can't hide from Him. We have to come to Him. I like the way the writer of Hebrews talks so much about how Jesus, as a man, though sinless, made a way for us to God. Because of what He did, we can "approach the throne of grace with confidence, so that we may receive mercy and find grace to help us in our time of need" (Heb. 4:16).

Sure, God sees everything. He sees our weaknesses. He sees the things we wrestle with. He sees how we stumble. He sees the thoughts that are awry. But we must constantly remember that, because of Jesus, God is forgiving—not accepting nor condemning—of the weaknesses, fears, temptations, and worries that color our imperfect, human selves.

We must "draw near to God with a sincere heart in full assurance of faith... [cleansed] from a guilty conscience" (Heb. 10:22). I believe that if we have a sincere heart and faith in Jesus, He calls us clean. Clean enough to come closer.

Come close enough to hear Him asking you to let Him shape your character. Hear Him offering to give you the power to be and do good. Hear Him call you to help Him make His world all that He dreams for it to be. You can be a moral leader who creates a God-inspired future. And our world needs leaders like you.

I want to share a story that makes me a little uncomfortable. But I think it's important for you to see that even pastors who write books about living our best lives have moments—maybe even some years—of struggle and doubt. Now, look. I am not a midlife crisis kind of guy. I'm a faith guy. I'm a let's-go-do-this-thing, let's-conquer-the-world kind of guy.

But a couple years ago, I realized that time is starting to run out. It was a weird thing. For years, everything seemed to be ahead of me. Then all of a sudden, everything seemed to be mostly behind me. I thought I'd be a whole lot further along in life—whatever that means—by now. Here I was, forty-five–forty-six years old. And for a year and a half—maybe two—I found myself feeling...disappointed. What happened?

There were big things. There were petty things. Like this: After years of working toward the vision of building a ministry in the New York City metropolitan area, we were still bottlenecked in far too small a building with very little parking. And all the things involved in building the new campus we needed in order to serve our busting-at-the-seams congregation and the communities around us seemed to be taking forever. Raising capital. Zoning and planning battles. "Not-in-my-backyard" neighbors.

I felt like Bill Murray in the movie *Groundhog Day*, getting up day after endless day saying the same words and fighting the same battles with little ever changing. I wondered how long my congregation would hang in there with me and our leadership as we fought for something we felt God had inspired us to do but which always seemed to be just out of our reach. I mean, c'mon! How much hair would I have to lose to see this thing happen already?!

Minor things. Major things. Maybe this whole New York thing was a pipe dream. Maybe I should have pastored a church where people seemed to actually want churches and want to get up on Sunday mornings and go listen to sermons. Maybe I shouldn't even be a pastor. I felt like a failure.

And then there was this book I'd written. *This* book. I had a message I wanted to share, but repeatedly, publishers said that though they loved it, I wasn't well known enough to take the risk. Not in this troubled economic and publishing climate. Thanks a lot. Repeated rejection.

Twenty-five-plus years of marriage. A beautiful, wonderful marriage to a woman I love with every fiber of my being. But we all know marriage is hard work at its best. And the intense infatuation of the honeymoon stage was, well, twenty-five years ago. What's going on?

Adult kids—kids who used to have to ask permission to leave the table—now they're out, making their own decisions, some of them good, and some of them decisions I wouldn't have made.

What happened? I found myself complaining. Not all the time, and really only to God, a really close friend, and—God bless her—my wife.

Let me be clear: this crisis wasn't about wanting a red Porsche convertible or some of the other stereotypical midlife wants. At least, not primarily. This crisis was about wanting my life to mean something. Something more! I wanted to know that my life mattered—a lot! I wanted a sense of significance that I felt I still hadn't achieved, and time was running out.

Then I went on a study break. Sharon and I stayed with my parents in their lovely home, nestled in the middle of six acres of wild and wonderful West Virginian woods. My dad had created an outdoor chapel on his property, and I loved to pray and think and read there. In the solace of that place, I read a simple story that became the mitigating factor in this crisis of self. It is an apocryphal story about Jesus and the disciples written by Elisabeth Elliot.[1]

Here's the story.

One day, Jesus woke up and said to His disciples, "I want you to do something, and I want you to do it for Me. I want you to pick up a rock. I want you to carry it, and I want you to follow Me." So the disciples go and each find a rock, and Peter—well, he was Peter. He found the smallest rock he could find, and that was what he carried.

Around lunchtime, Jesus instructed the men to put down their rocks. They complied, and with a wave of His hand, Jesus turned the rocks to bread. Lunch was served, and Peter's lasted all of about five seconds.

After lunch, Jesus again told them He wanted them to do something for Him. He wanted them to carry a rock. Well, as you can imagine, Peter found the biggest rock he could find and lugged that boulder around with him wherever Jesus went! All day long, he struggled with that rock, doing everything he could just to keep up.

Eventually, they came to a river. Jesus told them to throw their rocks into the river, and then said, "C'mon! Let's go!"

You can imagine what Peter thought. "Uhhh, hello? Lord?" he said. "I'm hungry. I carried my rock, just like You asked. I threw it in the river, just as You commanded." A pause. "It was a big rock!"

And Jesus turned to him and said, "Peter . . . *who were you carrying that rock for?*"

I had an epiphany when I read that story in those West Virginia woods. I realized that there was a part of me that was carrying my rock for myself. Somehow, without my wanting it to, it had become about me. I immediately marched into the house and said to Sharon, "I have an announcement to make. I am no longer in a midlife crisis."

And I wasn't.

Who was I doing this for? Who was I leading for? My job is ultimately to play the role God assigned to me! My job is to get out of bed every day and do what He asks me to do, where He asks me to do it. Who am I to be disappointed?

I believe for a lot of things. I expect them to happen. A lot of the things I have believed for have happened. But even if the things I believe for don't happen exactly the way I wanted, I don't have the right to be angry. Not if I've played the role God has asked me to play. My job is to carry the rock . . . for Him.

Who are you carrying your rock for?

In your quest to have a true heart and to be a virtuous person and a moral leader who helps create a better world, remember who your primary Audience is. Remember the One you must do this for.

Somebody is watching you. And that somebody can be the people around you who expect you to live up to your legend. That's OK—those people will help keep you honest. But, more importantly, that Somebody is the God who made you. He knows everything about you, even all those things that are in you that those other somebodies can't see. He knows that you wonder if you have the right stuff in you. If you can be the kind of person who has the moral fortitude to achieve truly great things. If you can measure up to your own or other people's expectations.

But ultimately, we have to measure up to His. He is who we're leading for. And that's good. Because He is cheering His heart out. He knows everything about us, and is still for us! And if God is for us…

Part Six

Reflection Questions

1. Consider this statement: "A moral future is an inclusive one.... If
    we are moral people, we cannot *not* be a leader." Does this statement
    make you uncomfortable or excited? Why?

2. Some people may not be naturally gifted with mercy, but this doesn't
    mean they are excused from being merciful. In the same way, people
    whose strengths are in areas other than leadership still aren't excused
    from leading. How can you develop leadership skills in your area
    of gifting so you can lead yourself and others to the best possible
    future?

3. What are some of the ways you feel unworthy to partner with God
    and to be a leader? Read 1 Corinthians 4:3–5. What will happen
    when God looks inside you and sees your motives? What are your
    concerns? What are those things that you believe God will praise?

4. "Moral leadership is to inspire, influence, and empower others to
    self-actualization and the accomplishment of mission." In light of
    this definition, what is your greatest strength? Where can you stand
    to improve?

Part Seven

LET'S GO THERE

Chapter 27
Stuff Happens

SEVERAL YEARS AGO, I was asked to cast vision to a group of New York City leaders about an important new leadership initiative in our region. The Willow Creek Association was partnering with an arm of Concerts of Prayer—Greater New York, which has since become the New York City Leadership Center, in an attempt to bring WCA's Global Leadership Summit to a number of satellite sites around the metropolitan area. I had been a part of the NYCLC team negotiating this and was now tasked to speak for a few minutes to some New York City–area pastors and leaders to articulate what this could mean for the region.

I was excited! This fit beautifully in my area of destiny. I was going to get to be a part of bringing a world-class leadership event to thousands of leaders in the most strategic city/region in the world. Furthermore, I was going to get to hang out with leaders from the city whom I admire, as well as the executive team of the WCA, several of whom would be speaking too. Win. Win. Win.

It was an incredibly hot and humid summer day. I made the stupid mistake of working out on the treadmill until the last possible minute before I had to shower and dress in a jacket and tie. A few minutes later, I was sitting in a poorly air-conditioned New Jersey Transit train, making the short commute to Manhattan. The meeting was being held at the headquarters of the venerable Bowery Mission at Madison and 31st.

I was still sweating like I was on the treadmill. I was running late and had four New York City blocks to walk in the oppressive heat. Perspiring profusely. Anxious. Late. Heart racing. A little worried that I was going to screw this thing up...at least my part of it.

Andrew McCleese and Thomas Mahoney, two of my teammates at the time, were with me. We got off the train at Penn Station, jostled with the rush-hour crowd, ran up the stairs to 7th Avenue, and started moving quickly toward our destination.

It was at about West 32nd and 6th that the bird-cow found me. Out of the heavens came a mess of such magnitude that when it landed on the left lapel of my finely tailored blue jacket, it seemed that I was knocked off stride. Supposedly cows don't fly. So this had to be a bird-cow. It had evidently been eating enormous amounts of mustard and peppercorn and perhaps some kind of seaweed.

Hot. Collar soaked with sweat. Late. Nervous. And the left side of my blue jacket devastated. Seven million people on the island of Manhattan, and this bird-cow chose me.

I'll tell you how bad the moment felt. My normally jovial staff buddies, Andrew and Thomas, didn't even laugh. The future was at stake, and the guy who was supposed to be speaking to it was a mess.

We started frantically looking for a place to get me cleaned up. They ran into a Dunkin' Donuts, looking for water, I guess. I saw a small courtyard and the open doors of a church immediately to my right. "A miracle!" I thought. I ran into what appeared, from my tradition or lack thereof, to be the lobby. I was looking for the priest or a restroom. The hallways were gated, and I found neither.

Then I saw the fountain. It was beautiful, pouring water out of the wall into a perfectly formed, waist-level basin. Thank God! And no one else was there except Andrew and Thomas now bringing Dunkin' Donuts napkins to my rescue.

I stood at the basin and started dipping and rubbing. Hot. Sweaty. Late. Panicked. Thomas and Andrew stood watching as if I were performing heart transplant surgery. Then we became aware that there were other people in the room. I turned around mid-rub. There were people. They were lined up behind me. Confusion. Disorientation. Realization. Embarrassment.

I was cleaning up my mess in the holy water!

Utter humiliation. By the looks on the faces of those lined up behind me, I'd egregiously offended a number of the faithful in one of the world's great religions. Sorry.

I did finally get there. At the door, I was greeted by my friend Steve Bell, executive vice president of the WCA, who insisted on hugging me and, as a much shorter man than I, perfectly planted his smiling face in the large wet and still a little yellow spot on the left lapel of my jacket. Sorry.

Just so you know, I found a quiet place and got cleaned up and cooled down and was able to participate in an evening that has helped bring leadership training to thousands of leaders in our region in the last several years.

Here's the point: Stuff happens on the way to your destiny. All kinds of stuff. Some of it—probably a lot of it—is what I call "lowercase *s*" stuff, at least in the big picture. The boss doesn't like you and won't promote you. A star employee decides to take her talent elsewhere. The coach likes another player at your position better than you for some reason known only to him. You battle with a chronic but treatable illness. The tenants damage your house. Your industry undergoes intractable changes. The neighbors oppose your building project. One of your kids has a learning disability. Then there are those seasons where all kinds of bad stuff seems to just fall out of the sky. You attempt to make it better but make it worse. But trust me. If you'll just keep moving forward, you'll get there. And at some point you might even laugh about some of the "small *s*" stuff.

Then there's the "uppercase *S*" stuff. My friend Chris Maxwell was pastoring a church, writing articles and curriculum, coaching basketball, and enjoying life. He and his wife had three sons. Chris had always been healthy. Healthy until March 1996.

After days of a fever, a struggle to communicate, and repeatedly fainting, Chris was rushed to the ER. They thought he had overdosed on drugs. He hadn't, of course. But his life was about to radically change.

Chris was suffering from encephalitis—it was slowly destroying his brain and taking his life. Slowly, painfully, miraculously, Chris recovered. But he would never be the same. He had been a great leader with a powerful intellect and a prodigious memory. He had memorized entire books of the Bible. Before March 1996.

Now he had brain damage—left temporal lobe—with major memory loss. He now lives with epilepsy. At first, he struggled to remember the names of his three sons.

Debbie, his wife of now twenty-nine years, was interviewed on the *700 Club* and called Chris "her second husband." He had changed that much. Speech therapy, hard work, medical care, the patience of his congregation, a stubbornness to not give up, and a loving family moved Chris forward. The doctors are amazed. Neurologists look at his MRI results and see major scar tissue. They can't believe he is traveling all over the world, writing and speaking to give hope to others experiencing life disappointments.

No, he's not the same man as the former Chris. He still struggles with his memory, and his basic personality has changed. But now he is actually better. Better at leading more people. Better at working as a team player. Better at understanding the struggles of others. And better at depending on God—the One whose strength is made perfect in Chris's weaknesses.

Yes, stuff will happen on the way to your destiny. Some of it is troubling, difficult, and challenging but manageable. Then there are those other things that appear to change everything. Maybe even unspeakable things. But if God called you to actualize what He's dreamed for you, you are going to get there somehow. It may not look exactly like you thought it would. It may not happen as quickly as you had hoped. You might be a different person when you finally arrive. But you are going to get there.

Moving from where we are to where we're called to go is going to be challenging. Trying to make a difference—change things—is always challenging. I like what former Federal Communications Commission head Michael Powell said when discussing the shift from the old to the new digital technology: "It will be messy and it will be confusing, and we will get a lot of it wrong and we will have to start over. But that's the creative process."[1]

That statement could be made about most change efforts in our lives. When we start to bring significant transformation of any kind—to make the future is different than our present in substantive ways—it usually begins a wonderfully messy adventure, oftentimes confusing and frequently full of both deep pain and great joy. I think some of us naively get on the path to our future and get surprised by the constant "three steps forward and two steps back" reality. The way to our God-inspired future is not a perfect linear process. Nor is it the straight line depicted by an organizational change graph, inevitably ascending toward what is better, best, and preferred. It looks more like the graph depicted below. The path to the future is a squiggly line.

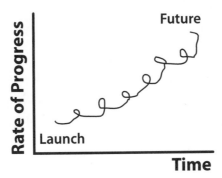

Great change takes great courage. I want to intensify your courage. As has been said in many ways by many others, courage is not the absence of fear. Traveling to your future will demand countless courageous thoughts, plans, and actions in the presence of doubt and anxiety and discouragement. You must take courage with you to your God-inspired future.

John Adams knew that America existed even prior to the actions that brought about its formation: "But what do we mean by the American Revolution? Do we mean the American War? The Revolution was affected before the war commenced. The Revolution was in the hearts and minds of the people."[2] But neither Adams nor his fellows entered into the creation of the United States without deep introspection, self-doubt, and even fear. As he traveled to the First Continental Congress in 1774, "many days he suffered intense torment over his ability to meet the demands of the new role to be played."[3] Adams wrote in the privacy of his diary, "I wander alone, and ponder. I muse, I mope, I ruminate...We have not men fit for the times. We are deficient in genius, education, in travel, fortune—in everything. I feel unutterable anxiety."[4]

This man who became one of the great figures in history knew the future was in him yet wondered if he would get there. He questioned himself. He questioned the capabilities of his colleagues—men like George Washington, Thomas Jefferson, and Benjamin Franklin. This seems unbelievable in retrospect. The great John Adams doubting himself? Doubting the abilities of Washington, Jefferson, and Franklin? Yes! This is typical of the kinds of questions people ask themselves as they embark on a revolutionary journey.

Perhaps you've had similar doubts about yourself and even those around you. But I want you to see greatness in yourself and the potential for greatness in everyone and everything around you. God wants to use you to create a new world.

Chapter 28

Take Courage with You

THERE IS A GREAT story in the New Testament book of Acts about Paul, one of the most influential leaders of the Christian church. Since becoming a follower of Jesus, Paul had spent a number of years traveling around the world preaching, planting churches, and writing what is now about a third of the New Testament. His potent influence had so threatened the power structure of religious Judaism and even the Roman Empire that he was arrested in Jerusalem by Roman officials at the request of his Jewish brothers. When the Romans could not find any cause to keep him imprisoned, Paul was released into the custody of the Jewish Council and given the opportunity to plead his case.

As he skillfully argued for his faith in Christ and the resurrection of the dead, the crowd erupted:

> The dispute became so violent that the commander was afraid Paul would be torn to pieces by them. He ordered the troops to go down and take him away from them by force and bring him into the barracks. The following night the Lord stood near Paul and said, '*Take courage!* As you have testified about me in Jerusalem, so you must also testify in Rome.'
>
> —Acts 23:10–11, EMPHASIS ADDED

These words would define much of the rest of Paul's life. God had given him a new assignment. He was saying, "I now have plans for you to go to the most influential city in the world, Rome. I want you to stand before Caesar, the most powerful man in the world, and share the Good News with him. Paul, I'm telling you that even though you feel like you are about to be torn apart, I have great plans for you. And know this: You are going to need to take courage with you." It is over two years before Paul actually arrives in Rome. Acts 23–28 gives highlights of his circuitous journey. Paul's path to the future was certainly a squiggly line. I have extracted five understandings from this story. I'll address two in this chapter and three in the following chapter.

One: Focus on Your Future. Central to Paul maintaining courage was his certainty about his destination. He always remembered that he was called to go to Rome. I think that the inevitable detours we experience as we move toward our futures are less onerous when we have a clear view of our landing place. It is so compelling to know what your life is supposed to be about. I want to repeat that you can know your place of destiny, practice the discipline of imagining within it, act accordingly, and lead others to their destined places. The importance of constantly remembering what you have been called to do cannot be overstated. You have to know where you are going.

No other options existed for Paul but getting to Rome. There were times when he could have been set free to take another path. One example of this is that, after receiving death threats in Jerusalem, government officials transferred Paul to Caesarea where he remained imprisoned for two years awaiting a hearing. While there, Paul mentored a certain Roman governor named Felix. Felix hoped that Paul or one of his followers would pay a large bribe, after which he would set Paul free. That was not Paul's style. He did not want to be released. Prison surely had its difficulties, but prison was part of his path to Rome. Felix was then succeeded by a man named Festus. Festus quickly granted Paul a trial and brought in the Roman-appointed Jewish king, Herod Agrippa, to oversee the legal proceedings.

Paul was a Roman citizen. It was quite a privilege to have Roman citizenship during that period of history, and it entitled Paul the right to appeal to Caesar. In this trial, he exercised this right when he answered Festus, "If I have done something worthy of death, I don't refuse to die. But if I am innocent, no one has a right to turn me over to these men to kill me. I appeal to Caesar!" (Acts 25:11, NLT). Festus and Herod Agrippa announced that they would have released Paul, but because he petitioned to go to Rome, they were not able to. Paul was now stuck on the path to Rome, but he was stuck on purpose. He made this decision in line with his destiny.

I've noticed that a lot of people want to keep all their options open when they contemplate their future. I think that this is wisdom in some cases. But when you know what you have been called to do, then Plan A should be your only plan. When Sharon and I moved from the Midwest of our upbringing to the New York City metropolitan area nineteen years ago, we were as certain as two human beings could be that this was our place of destiny. We made this area our home in every way. There was no Plan B. There is no way to underestimate the implications of this mindset of every area of our lives. I realize that we could have some new, defining word that would move us to a different place and a different future, but until then, every decision we make is in line with what we believe God has called us to do here. There are no options.

A couple of weeks ago, I was having a conversation with a thirty-something single man about the nature of his relationship with a young woman with whom I always see him. I said, "What's going on with you and _____?" He said, "I know I'm going to have to do something about this. I believe that she's the one, but I always like to keep my options open." Then he said something I love to hear: "A few weeks ago, I heard you do this message about Paul and how when he knew what he was supposed to do, he deliberately shut every other door. That talk messed me up. I now know that I have to make a commitment. I know that she's the one. I know that there can never be anyone else."

I can pretty much assure you that a number of times on the path to your God-inspired future, attractive alternatives will be offered. You will be presented with more money, or a better position, or a more sedate lifestyle in a more comfortable geographical location. You are going to face other kinds of more dramatic temptations as well. We all do. But we have to constantly remember our future. There are no other options.

Enemies always come along with success. People both appreciate strength and success in others; for the same reasons, strong, successful people are both admired and attacked.

—Carly Fiorina,
Tough Choices[1]

Two: Starve Your Enemies. The day after the Lord told Paul to take courage with him to this new place in his life, his enemies "formed a conspiracy and bound themselves with an oath not to eat or drink until they had killed [him]. More than forty men were involved in this plot" (Acts 23:12–13). Wow! Most of us know that as sure as we have a God-inspired future, there are forces that conspire to keep us from it. Our dreams always have enemies.

This is what has occurred to me as I've read this passage over the years: These guys who had sworn to not eat or drink until they killed Paul must have gotten very hungry. About four days into this pact, they either drank or died. Their plans against Paul were not in agreement with God's plans for Paul, so it didn't matter what kind of oath they made. They either starved to death or became publicly known, certifiable liars. I love the imagery. We must learn how to starve our enemies.

Now, there are several of ways to do this. First, you have to have good intelligence. When Paul became aware that his enemies had schemed to kill him, he alerted the commander, who devised a plan to save him.

You need to know that you are going to have enemies. Some of these enemies are human beings; then there are the spiritual forces behind human beings. You have to prepare for this certainty and not be shocked when inevitable opposition rolls your way. Don't be disheartened when you have a dream, a sense of calling, an understanding of your destiny, and all kinds of forces around you seem to conspire to stop it all.

Most any worthy change effort brings opposition. Leaders are frequently warned that their efforts to bring change to organizations or individuals will bring resistance, perhaps from the very people the leader is most trying to help. Why? That's just how people are. Sometimes even the most well-intentioned people are just intimidated by change. They are not evil. They are just not as courageous as you, or maybe they don't have the clear picture of the future that you do.

Then there are a lot of petty and small-minded people out there who wrestle with jealousy and cringe at the thought of you being successful. While they should probably be patting you on the back, they are instead talking about you around the water cooler. But that's okay. Just have good intelligence; know those folks exist. Truth be told, it has taken me years to accept this and I still don't like it one bit.

Let's explore the other dimension of opposition that comes from a place of dark spirituality. Some opposition is natural, but some is supernatural. In Ephesians 6, we are warned that we are not just fighting against human beings, but against forces outside of ourselves. We are encouraged to protect ourselves so that we can stand against such enemies: "For we are not fighting against flesh-and-blood enemies, but against evil rulers and authorities of the unseen world, against mighty powers in this dark world, and against evil spirits in the heavenly places" (Eph. 6:12, NLT). There are dark powers that influence this world that I don't completely understand. But I know this: there are times when you feel that hell just broke loose, and it's possible that it did. You have spiritual adversaries who do not want you to help create a better future for yourself or anyone else.

We should be wise not to give our enemies opportunities to thwart our God-given plans. Scripture reminds us that we should not give evil a foothold (Eph. 4:27). We have to be very careful to guard ourselves from those areas of vulnerability that beg the question, "If my enemies were to try to mess me up, what might they find in me?" What areas in our lives would give our enemies a stronghold from which to attack us? What bad habits do we have? What negative thoughts are running through our heads? Are we harboring unforgiveness? Are we bitter? Are we sloppy with our finances? Do we have poor planning skills? There are potentially all kinds of things in us that our enemies could have on us. These are things they can feed on. We must starve our enemies. We must give them nothing to use against us. Jesus said, "The prince of this world is coming. He has no hold on me" (John 14:30). I want this to be true of me.

We also can defeat our enemies by learning how to fight when necessary. The way we fight darkness, though, is not through physical means, but through spiritual power: "For though we live in the world, we do not wage war as the world does. The weapons we fight with are not the weapons of the world. On the contrary, they have divine power to demolish strongholds" (2 Cor. 10:3–4). This is a critical truth! When people oppose you, do not retaliate against them. Fight against the spiritual influences that stand behind them. Learn to be strong in the Spirit. Learn to be strong in the Scriptures. Learn to be strong in prayer. Learn to be strong in praise. Learn to be strong in community. Learn to be strong in purpose. If you learn these things, then your enemies won't mess with you for long.

I also have discovered that it disarms our enemies when we keep moving toward our God-dreams in spite of the turbulence that is always swirling around change leaders. There is incredible power in just getting up every day and working toward our God-inspired futures. I know I have frustrated the life out of some of the people that have opposed me by just showing up again and again and talking about my vision with a smile on my face, energy in my step, and faith in my heart.

Our church has gone through lengthy and difficult battles in front of zoning and planning boards and, in one case, the West Orange town council. In each instance, we were making application regarding our need to expand or relocate our facilities to serve more people. Though we ultimately won overwhelming approval in each instance, these victories never came without tremendous resistance from some in our community who have a different picture than we do of the future of our township and our church's role in it.

Many years ago, we were applying to convert a former bowling-alley-turned-printing-factory into a worship center. Our church was relatively unknown at that point, and a cacophony of neighbors organized to oppose us for any number of stated reasons. In retrospect, I think most of them were fine people who were just afraid of the unknown and totally unaware of the negative spiritual energy being manifested through their opposition. Most of the people of this New York City suburb have never witnessed a multiethnic, multiracial, multigenerational, nondenominational church thrive and grow and constantly attempt to expand its physical facilities.

We appeared again and again before the zoning board over six intense months. During this time, someone anonymously published some terrible lies about me and our church and distributed them all over the area. People stood up in public meetings and said awful things and asked me about every specious question you can imagine. Finally, the zoning board,

God bless it, chose to believe the truth, judge the case on its legal merits, and voted to approve our application.

As I write this now, I am fresh from a similar battle, this time before the planning board. We made application to erect offices as the first step in the development of our new church campus, which is located on the opposite side of town from our present worship center. Again, some folks in our new neighborhood anonymously published a new series of lies about us and distributed it in the areas around our new campus. Someone called a reporter and anonymously spread vicious untruths. People sent letters to the editor to oppose us. The public meetings again found people making strong statements against us for any number of reasons. Many questions were posed. Some were legitimate, like, "Will this church have enough parking?" The private sidebars were more revealing. One woman asked with disdain, "Are you going to bring more African Americans into this neighborhood?" Interestingly, several front-page articles and a lead television news story about our church were positive. Public relations and sentiment turned strongly in our favor.

When it came time for the planning board to finally vote, the first two board members quickly voted yes. The third guy made a short speech before his vote. He said that I probably didn't remember him, but that perhaps I should. Fifteen years earlier, when our application for our worship center was before the zoning board, he was the spokesman for a group of neighbors who opposed our application. It was to no avail because ultimately our application was approved. But, he went on, since that time he had carefully watched our church as it grew in that location. He noticed that we kept all the promises that we had made to the community. He was impressed with the kind of people our church attracted and the positive impact we made on the neighborhood. And then he said that he has every reason to believe that the same will be true as it concerned this application and our future development in this new location. He then voted yes, and so did every other member of the board—a unanimous decision.

All I had really done to turn an "enemy" into a friend, and this unknowingly, was to get up every day, year after year, and lead our congregation to be who we said we were and do what we said we would do. We just kept building toward the better future we said we believed in.

Many times over the years I have had people who opposed us that first time express how much they appreciate what we have meant to the community and how much they regret resisting us. I believe with all my heart that some of those folks who are trying to stop our dreams now will become friends in the future. We just have to keep consistently creating the eventualities that we are fighting for.

If you find yourself all bloodied and bruised by those who are antagonistic toward your vision of the future, do not underestimate the power of just showing up day after day. Starve your enemies. Drive your opposition nuts. When possible, make your opponents your friends. Just keep moving forward.

"Hey Paul, where are you going?"
"I'm going to Rome."

Chapter 29
We Will Get There

You will get to your future. But you have to keep your courage even when things go wrong. And they will.

Three: Keep Your Courage Even When Things Go Wrong. After two years in prison, Paul finally set out for Rome, accompanied by a Roman centurion and a small company of soldiers. They planned to put him on a succession of ships from Caesarea to Rome, along the western coast of the province of Asia. As they got ready to board a ship at a port in Fair Havens, Crete, Paul had a strong spiritual intuition that there was going to be a tremendous gale that would ultimately cause the ship to go down. He warned his escorts accordingly. Instead of listening to the preacher, however, they listened to the weather prognosticator and the captain. They literally set sail into a mistake of biblical proportions:

> The majority decided that we should sail.... When a gentle south wind began to blow, they thought they had obtained what they wanted; so they weighed anchor and sailed along the shore of Crete. Before very long, a wind of hurricane force, called the "northeaster," swept down from the island.
>
> —Acts 27:12–14

It became extremely dark, and they were barely able to secure their boat. They actually took ropes and passed them under and around the ship to prevent it from breaking apart. They also lowered the anchor, but the wind was so powerful it dragged the anchor along like a rag doll. The men then threw all the cargo overboard. On the third day, they finally tossed the ship's tackle overboard. There was nothing else they could do. In the middle of this terrible situation, Paul had an I-told-you-so moment. He said to his fatigued and frightened companions, "Men, you should have taken my advice not to sail from Crete; then you would have spared yourselves this damage and loss" (v. 21).

While Paul could have rubbed it in further, he didn't. Instead he explained, "But now I urge you to *keep up your courage*, because not one of you will be lost; only the ship will be destroyed. Last night an angel of the God whose I am and whom I serve stood beside me and said, 'Do not be afraid, Paul. You must stand trial before Caesar; and God has graciously given you the lives of all who sail with you.' So *keep up your courage*, men, for I have faith in God that it will happen just as he told me. Nevertheless, we must run aground on some island" (vv. 22–26, EMPHASIS ADDED).

This passage intrigues me. Sometimes we shipwreck because the people around us won't listen. But let's be real. We usually crash and burn because we don't listen to God, or the people He sends to protect us, or that gut instinct that warns us on an intuitive level of an impending disaster. Most of the messes we end up in are repercussions of dumb human mistakes. Even on the way to our God-inspired future.

At some juncture, we make a decision that propels us into the harrowing winds of confusion, and controversy, and consternation. Try as we might to put an anchor down, or stop the leaking, or salvage the situation, we find ourselves fortunate to have a splintered board from our shattered situation that keeps us from drowning. Exhausted, we have just enough something to get to the next place, lick our wounds, assess the damage, and start making plans about how to get to our destination.

If you are on one of those shipwreck detours that cause you to feel like you deserve to go down, if you are grasping onto pieces of wood in the middle of a raging ocean, if you are desperately swimming or treading water trying to find a dry place—listen to the voice of God saying, "Keep your courage. I still have the same plans for you that I had before I created you. Have faith in me. It will happen just as I told you."

Maybe you hired the wrong person. Maybe you underestimated the costs in a planning process. Maybe you were too hasty in making an executive call. If God aborted every future He inspired when the inspired person made a mistake and nearly drowned, then no one would have a future.

In Paul's story, some of us might have expected God to show up in anger and say to the bull-headed men, "I'm going to bust this boat up and kill you all because you are a bunch of fools. You should have listened to what I was saying through Paul in the first place." But God didn't give them an "I-told-you-so" speech. In our own similar experiences, God does not say that to us. He is likely whispering, "I am with you. Now, take the time to understand how you got here. Let Me help you make things right. Let's rebuild this broken mess, and then let's go. Let's go to your future."

The other day I spoke to a pastor for whom I have a great deal of respect. Years ago, he led his congregation into a very ambitious campus development project. Along the way, he made some business decisions that people around him who love him cautioned him against. There was nothing evil or underhanded about any of these decisions. They revolved around how to finance the project, whom to hire to oversee it, assumptions about the economy, things like that. Right now, the project appears dead. And because of some of the ways he conducted business, his own home is in foreclosure. It looks like a shipwreck.

He told me that he hasn't been sleeping much and that during the darkest moments in the night he rehearses some of those decisions he made. He knows now that he should have gone this way instead of that way. He should have listened more to the people around him. You know the kind of thoughts he's having. We've all had them. But my prayer for this man is that he will keep his courage. That he will know that we are not defined by our mistakes. That he will grab ahold of whatever means God provides to get to a safe, dry place. I believe he will get himself together and get back on the journey to his future. God has no interest in incessant I-told-you-so's. God is interested in getting us to our destinies.

Four: Learn How to Shake Things Off. With everything Paul had gone through—being arrested, getting death threats, sitting in jail for years without a proper trial, and being shipwrecked—he washed up on an island called Malta. He and the rest of his wet and weary shipmates were warmly welcomed by the natives. Someone started a bonfire. As Paul gathered a pile of brush to kindle the flames, a viper came out of nowhere and sank its poisonous fangs into his hand. What else could have gone wrong?

> When the islanders saw the snake hanging from his hand, they said to each other, "This man must be a murderer; for though he escaped from the sea, Justice has not allowed him to live." But Paul *shook the snake off* into the fire and suffered no ill effects. The people expected him to swell up or suddenly fall dead, but after waiting a long time and seeing nothing unusual happen to him, they changed their minds and said he was a god.
>
> —Acts 28:4–6, EMPHASIS ADDED

So here Paul is, trying to steady himself and recover from the latest near tragedy, and a snake comes out of nowhere and bites him on the hand. The people around him act like people often do. They stand around waiting for him to keel over dead. And when he doesn't, they nearly worship him. One minute you're a nimrod, and the next minute you're a hero. One day they hate you, and the next day they love you. One day people are waiting for you to die, and the next day they're bowing down before your authority. Both extremes are ridiculous.

I hate being bitten by snakes. In the broad view of Paul's journey this appears to be, to him, a minor incident. He seems so certain of the "I'm going to Rome" thing and so inoculated from difficulty that he just "shook it off." I tend to be better at dealing with the big things—like avoiding shipwrecks—than I am with those serpentine little things. I can get a negative email about some minor point that sets me off in a major way. But Paul didn't sweat the small stuff. He just shook it off.

There are those things that happen that seem big at the time, but which you know are not going to kill you. You know what you should do when you just about get where you are going and a snake fastens itself to your hand? When a critic speaks against you? When a staff team member quits? When a negative news article comes out filled with misinformation? When it snows on a big weekend and you have to cancel your services—something I might have to do as I'm writing this? Just shake it off.

Five: Go Heal Somebody. What happened next?

> There was an estate nearby that belonged to Publius, the chief official of the island. He welcomed us to his home and for three days entertained us hospitably. His father was sick in bed, suffering from fever and dysentery. Paul went in to see him and, after prayer, placed his

hands on him and healed him. When this had happened, the rest of the sick on the island came and were cured. They honored us in many ways and when we were ready to sail, they furnished us with the supplies we needed.

—Acts 28:7–10

On your way to wherever you're going, despite the crash-and-burn episodes, despite what the enemy is doing, despite the storms and snakes, you have to make sure that you're always healing somebody. I'm told that one of the keys to recovery is to never be self-absorbed. You can't revolve your life around only yourself and your future. You need to make sure you are helping someone else recover as well. On your way to your destiny, make sure that the trip is never just about you. Go heal somebody.

The most important element of this story is that Paul got to where he was supposed to go. I think my favorite passage in this whole adventure is, "And so we came to Rome" (Acts 28:14). If you read that verse in a vacuum and didn't know the succession of turbulent events that took place during the preceding couple of years, you'd probably think, "So what?" With most success stories we hear, we are more attuned to the destination aspect rather than the journey part.

I love to read biographies about great leaders throughout history. What amazes me is the commonality of their experiences. I don't recall any of them just starting out with great success. There were risks. There were setbacks. There were losses. There were failures. There were temptations. There were long periods of time where nothing seemed to be going right.

Remember Abraham Lincoln's story? He endured a squiggly-line journey toward becoming the sixteenth president of the United States. He suffered from clinical depression and had two nervous breakdowns. He lost his first political battle when he ran for the Illinois State Assembly. While he was elected years later as an assemblyman and was eventually elected to the House of Representatives, he lost a bid for the United States Senate. Lincoln's life sojourn wasn't about immediate success. It was joyful and painful. It was triumphant and sad. It was a journey. But many people view him only through the eyes of his final destination as one of the great presidents of a great nation.

Don't equate successful people with their ultimate successes without remembering the circuitous path they journeyed. What's the big deal in someone writing a best-selling book, or creating a Fortune 500 company, or finding a cure for a fatal disease? The big deal is usually the backstories, the stories that lie behind such remarkable achievements. If you stand discouraged at some point on your path to your future, know that the day will come when you will be able to say, "And so we came to Rome." Take courage. You're going to get there.

Chapter 30
Yes, We Will!

MOST OF US ARE in a place that is far less than what we believe is our God-inspired place. Some of us are in a mess. A broken place. Regardless, we are all in a huge reconstruction project. All of us are reconstructing the broken image of God in our lives, our families, and our communities. We are called to remake our world into what God imaged it to be.

This reminds me of the promise of Isaiah 61. God's people, to whom this was written, had just returned from years of exile. But they returned to a broken city. Jerusalem had been conquered decades earlier. The Jews were taken captive and exiled far from home—their city destroyed.

Zerubabel led the people from exile back to their broken city. But he wanted more.

Isaiah has him declare this:

> The Spirit of the Sovereign Lord is on me, because the Lord has anointed me to preach good news to the poor. He has sent me to bind up the brokenhearted, to proclaim freedom for the captives and release from darkness for the prisoners, to proclaim the year of the LORD's favor and the day of vengeance of our God, to comfort all who mourn, and provide for those who grieve in Zion—to bestow on them a crown of beauty instead of ashes, the oil of gladness instead of mourning, and a garment of praise instead of a spirit of despair.
>
> —Isaiah 61:1–3

This is wonderful stuff. This is a God-inspired future.

But then this leader says, "They will rebuild the *ancient ruins* and restore the *places long devastated;* they will renew the *ruined cities* that have been devastated for generations" (v. 4 EMPHASIS ADDED). This is a dose of present reality. The people had been delivered from exile but placed in a city that had to be reconstructed—ancient ruins, places long devastated, messed up for generations.

These folks had been set free, but they had been set free to a big wreck. Their homes were destroyed. The temple was a heap of rubble. The walls surrounding the city of Jerusalem had been torn down. They had no king and no army. Their promise of a future was given in the context of a mess.

Sometimes we tend to think that a promise of a better future mitigates years of past devastation and current destruction. We need to consider, though, that we've been set free to rebuild. The fact that Christ has come into our life or that God has made clear to us His dreams for our future doesn't mean that there isn't a tremendous amount of work to do. We have a long journey ahead of us.

In the poignantly honest words of a pastor trying to rebuild a broken marriage, he reveals his surprise at discovering how much the past had contributed to present pain:

> Underneath the surface, our marriage bore a striking resemblance to that of our parents. Gender roles; the handling of anger and conflict and shame; how we defined success; our view of family, children, recreation, pleasure, sexuality, grieving; and our relationships with friends had all been shaped by our families' origins and our cultures. Sitting in that counselor's office that day, embarrassed by the state of our marriage, we learned a lesson we would never forget: Even though we had been committed Christians for almost twenty years, our ways of relating mirrored much more our family of origin than the way God intended for His new family in Christ.[1]

Your personal or family life may not be a mess. I hope it's not. But all of our lives are lived in a broken world—ancient ruins. This influences so much of our thinking about everything around us, including what's possible for us. We have been delivered from exile to places long devastated. We've been delivered to brokenness. We've been delivered to poverty. We've been delivered to addiction. We've been delivered to sickness. We've been delivered to torn families. Don't be surprised that there's rubble all around. The Spirit of the Lord is on you to rebuild, to bring change, to cause the things around you—family, culture, church, business—to look more like the way God wants it to look.

You are a change agent. You are a leader. You *will* rebuild.

We must not get discouraged when all these things in us and around us are not magically fixed overnight. When the people of Israel were put back into their city, they didn't rebuild it in a few months. It was sixteen years before they got the temple rebuilt and decades before the entire city of Jerusalem was repaired. During these years, they struggled with their priorities and experienced a number of setbacks. On several occasions, God had to send prophets to stir them up and get them back on track. We must not constantly wonder if we're in the right place—whether that's a marriage, or a business, or a church—because success seems to be taking forever. Ancient ruins take time to rebuild.

I read an article about two dolphins in an aquarium in China who fell deathly ill after ingesting plastic. Several attempts were made to remove the plastic surgically, but they failed. In a last-ditch effort to save the dying dolphins, the veterinarians looked for help in an unusual source—a 7'9" herdsman from Inner Mongolia—the world's tallest man. His arms are 41.7 inches long, evidently the longest arms in the world. They transported him to the aquarium. He stuck his hands with his long arms through the mouth and into the stomach of each dolphin. He grabbed the plastic, pulled it out, and saved their lives.

I got to thinking about that story as it concerns Isaiah 61. Here are these people standing in the middle of those ruins wondering, "How in the world can we expect all of this to get fixed?" Then I remembered the passages leading up to this chapter, specifically a verse in Isaiah 59: "Surely the arm of the LORD is not too short to save" (v. 1). We can believe that God sees us in our present reality even as we're surrounded by the rubble of a broken world. He wants to reach His hand into whatever is broken and fix it. We are His hands, but ultimately we can expect to create new futures because God has the longest arms in the world. He can project Himself with all of His power into whatever place we are in and help us create a new reality. You will... because He will.

I believe with all my heart that each of us can experience life in all its fullness. More and better life than we ever dreamed of. We can move our lives from wherever we are toward a *TEN*. We can create a better future—the best possible future—for ourselves and others. We can have total fulfillment.

If we want to.

Part Seven
Reflection Questions

1. Remember this: "The way to our God-inspired future is not a perfect linear process." It's a messy adventure, a squiggly line on the way to our future where "stuff happens." What thoughts or experiences cross your mind when you hear that "stuff happens"—big or small— on the way to your destiny?

2. The discipline of constantly remembering what God has called us to do is key to maintaining courage on the way to our futures. What are some of the benefits of focusing on your future? How will doing so help when attractive alternatives arise?

3. There are forces or enemies that conspire to keep us from our God-inspired futures. How does knowing this help us to "starve our enemies"? According to the author, what are some of the ways to do this? Read 2 Corinthians 10:3–4. Who are your enemies, and how does this truth help you to change the way you "fight" against them?

4. Ponder this statement: "If God aborted every future He inspired when the inspired person made a mistake and nearly drowned, then no one would have a future." How does this truth impact you? What could you accomplish on the way to your destiny if you shed the lie that failure is final with God?

5. "Serpentine little things" will happen. Reflect upon the serpentine little things in your life. Does it look like receiving a negative email? Getting bad news? Rewrite your response to these things and see yourself "shaking them off." Remember that the road to your best future includes others. How can you "heal somebody" who struggles with the trials of everyday life?

6. Jesus said, "I came to give life—life in all its fullness" (John 10:10, NCV) or "more and better life than [you] ever dreamed of" (MSG). Using this Scripture verse as your guide, and having read *TEN*, how would you rate your life on a scale of one to *TEN*? What has changed? What remains the same? What's next for you?

Acknowledgments

THE PEOPLE OF THE Life Christian Church: You are the incubator for these ideas. Thank you for saying yes to possibility over and over again. It is impossible to describe my joy when I think of you. Thank you for your kindness to me and my family these past twenty years.

The Board (BOD) and Elders (PAC) at TLCC: Thanks for affording me the liberty to do things like write this book and for supporting me in this project in every conceivable way.

The Staff Team at TLCC: What a great team we are! Thank you for helping me serve our wonderful congregation and for helping to fulfill our mission to "inspire people to grow in their lives with God." To my creative staff team—Bart Dyer, David Smith, and Chris Holewski: your creativity helps make hard work fun and helped make this book concept better. To my internal *TEN* team—Kerry Connelly, Jose Gonzalez, and Aisha Irvis: thanks for helping me bring positive closure to this project in so many ways. And to Dawn Young, my executive assistant: you have served me and the rest of the team so well these past six years. You are fantastic.

To my Literary Team: Esther Fedorkevich: thanks for challenging me to write, and for working so hard to get the earlier version of this book published in a very challenging publishing environment. Mark Sweeney: thank you for believing in this project, taking up the challenge, and connecting me to HigherLife. Thanks to Amy Gregory and my editor,

237

Chris Maxwell. Thanks especially, Chris, for your excellent input and friendship.

To my Family: Sharon: thanks for cheering for me all these years, and for being someone I can cheer for. I am so grateful that we share life together. Sumerr, Caleb, and Christian: being your mom's husband and your dad is the most meaningful part of my life. Our family means everything to me. I believe in each of you and pray passionately that you each create the best possible future for yourselves and others. God-inspired futures.

To Jesus Christ: My life is filled with joy, and I acknowledge You as the source of it all—life and joy. Thank You. I offer this book and my life to You...again. I pray that it will help make Your dreams come true for everyone who reads it. Thank You for more and better life than I ever dreamed of.

Terry A. Smith
February 2011

Notes

Introduction: What Do You Want?

1. David McCullough, *John Adams* (New York: Simon & Schuster, 2001), 47.

2. Bill Clinton, remarks on the awarding of the Presidential Medal of Freedom to Frances Hesselbein, as quoted on Leader to Leader Institute, "Hesselbein Wins Presidential Medal of Freedom," accessed March 18, 2011, http://www.pfdf.org/about/press-releases-df_press_release.html.

Chapter 1: The Future Is in You

1. Thomas P. M. Barnett, *The Pentagon's New Map: War and Peace in the Twenty-First Century* (New York: G. P. Putnam's Sons, 2004), 8.

2. Ibid., 7.

3. Donald Miller, *A Million Miles in a Thousand Years: Things I Learned While Editing My Life* (Nashville: Thomas Nelson, 2009), 48.

4. Doris Kearns Goodwin, *Team of Rivals: The Political Genius of Abraham Lincoln* (New York: Simon & Schuster, 2005), 146.

5. Ibid., 719.

Chapter 2: High Hope Levels

1. John Naisbitt and Patricia Aburdene, *Reinventing the Corporation: Transforming Your Job and Your Company for the New Information Society* (New York: Warner Books, 1986).

Chapter 3: The Role You Were Made For

1. Francis A. Schaeffer, *True Spirituality: How to Live for Jesus Moment by Moment* (Carol Stream, IL: Tyndale, 2001), 104.

2. W. E. Vine, Merrill F. Unger, and William White Jr., *An Expository Dictionary of Biblical Words* (Nashville: Thomas Nelson, 1985).

Chapter 4: Created to Transcend

1. James W. Sire, *The Universe Next Door*, 5th ed. (Downers Grove, IL: InterVarsity, 2009), 32.

2. Viktor E. Frankl, *Man's Search for Meaning* (Boston: Beacon, 2006), 76.

3. Vishal Mangalwadi, foreword to Darrow L. Miller with Stan Guthrie, *Discipling Nations: The Power of Truth to Transform Cultures* (Seattle: YWAM, 2001).

4. Osho, *God Is Dead: Now Zen Is the Only Living Truth* (India: Rebel, 1997).

Chapter 5: Created to Create

1. Dallas Willard, *The Divine Conspiracy: Rediscovering Our Hidden Life in God* (New York: HarperCollins, 1998), 81.

2. Michael Novak, *The Spirit of Democratic Capitalism* (Boulder, CO: Madison, 1990).

3. Douglas Jones and Douglas Wilson, *Angels in the Architecture: A Protestant Vision for Middle Earth* (Moscow, ID: Canon, 1998), 25.

Chapter 6: Naming Possibility

1. Philip Yancey, *Disappointment with God: Three Questions No One Asks Aloud* (Grand Rapids, MI: Zondervan, 1992), 60.

2. Eugene H. Peterson, *The Contemplative Pastor: Returning to the Art of Spiritual Direction* (Grand Rapids, MI: Wm. B. Eerdmans, 1993),102–105.

3. John Calvin, *The Institutes of Christian Religion* 3.20.3.

Chapter 7: Travel in God's Mind

1. J. I. Packer, *Knowing God* (Downers Grove, IL: InterVarsity, 1993).

2. Bono and The Edge, "Miracle Drug," from *How to Dismantle an Atomic Bomb*, 2004.

Chapter 8: See What God Sees

1. Wayne Grudem, *Systematic Theology: An Introduction to Biblical Doctrine* (Grand Rapids, MI: Zondervan, 1994), 702.

Chapter 9: God's Self-Limitation

1. Jack Hayford, *Prayer Is Invading the Impossible* (Gainesville, FL: Bridge-Logos, 2002), 157.

2. Dorothy Sayers, as quoted in Philip Yancey and Paul Brand, *In His Image* (Grand Rapids, MI: Zondervan, 1984), 137.

3. John Wesley, as quoted in Peter C. Wagner, *Prayer Shield* (Ventura, CA: Regal, 1992), 29.

4. Willard, *The Divine Conspiracy*, 76.

5. Dr. Karl Menninger, MD, with Martin Mayman, PhD, and Paul Pruyser, PhD, *The Vital Balance* (New York: Viking, 1963), 22.

Chapter 10: Positive Audaciousness

1. Peter Robinson, *How Ronald Reagan Changed My Life* (New York: HarperCollins, 2003), 119.

2. Ibid., 119–120.

3. Ibid., 119, emphasis added.

4. Jim Collins and Jerry I. Porras, *Built to Last: Successful Habits of Visionary Companies* (New York: HarperCollins, 1997), 94.

5. Ibid., 93.

6. Richard Foster, *Celebration of Discipline: The Path to Spiritual Growth* (New York: Harper & Row, 1978), 22.

7. Ibid.

8. Ibid.

9. Norman Vincent Peale, *Positive Imaging: The Powerful Way to Change Your Life* (New York: Ballantine, 1982), 17.

Chapter 11: Creative Audaciousness

1. Matthew Henry, *Bible Knowledge Commentary* (Elgin, IL: David C. Cook, 2002).

Chapter 12: Prophetic Audaciousness

1. William Backus, PhD, *Telling the Truth to Troubled People: A Manual for Christian Counselors* (Bloomington, MN: Bethany House, 1985), 59.

2. Ronald B. Adler and Russell F. Proctor, *Looking Out, Looking In,* 13th ed. (Boston: Wadsworth, Cengage Learning, 2011), 60.

3. Robert Rosenthal, PhD, and Lenore Jacobsen, EdD, *Pygmalion in the Classroom: Teacher Expectation and Pupils' Intellectual Development* (Norwalk, CT: Crown House, 1992).

4. Darrow, *Discipling the Nations*, 116.

Chapter 13: Refined Audaciousness

1. M. Scott Peck, *The Road Less Traveled and Beyond: Spiritual Growth in an Age of Anxiety* (New York: Touchstone, 1997), 13.

2. Daniel Defoe, *Robinson Crusoe*, First Aladdin Paperbacks ed. (New York: Aladdin Paperbacks, 2001), 101–102.

3. Jim Collins, *Good to Great: Why Some Companies Make the Leap...and Others Don't* (New York: HarperCollins, 2001), 80ff.

4. Vincent Normal Peale, *The True Joy of Positive Living: An Autobiography* (New York: Harper Perennial, 1998).

5. Max DePree, *Leadership Jazz: The Essential Elements of a Great Leader* (New York: Doubleday, 2008), 110–111.

Chapter 14: Not Always This Way

1. Goodwin, *Team of Rivals*, 87.

2. Ibid., ix.

3. As quoted by J. F. Snyder, president of the Illinois State Historical Society, who interviewed men under Lincoln's command.

4. Benjamin P. Thomas, *Abraham Lincoln: A Biography* (Carbondale, IL: Southern Illinois University Press, 2008), 133.

5. Dave Marum, Steve Smith, and Mahan Khalsa, *Business Think: 8 Rules for Getting It Right—Now and No Matter What!* (New York: John Wiley & Sons, 2002), 33.

Chapter 15: Theory Y God

1. Douglas MacGregor, *Adventure in Thought and Action,* Proceedings of the Fifth Anniversary Convocation of the School of Industrial Management, Massachusetts Institute of Technology, Cambridge, April 9, 1957.

2. Ibid.

3. Paul Hersey, Kenneth H. Blanchard, and Dewey E. Johnson, *Management of Organizational Behavior: Leading Human Resources,* 8th ed. (Upper Saddle River, NJ: Prentice-Hall, 2001), 61.

4. Peter Scazzero, *Emotionally Healthy Spirituality: Unleash the Power of Authentic Life in Christ* (Nashville: Thomas Nelson, 2006); and Scazzero, *The Emotionally Healthy Church: A Strategy for Discipleship that Actually Changes Lives* (Grand Rapids, MI: Zondervan, 2010).

5. Barbara R. Bjorkland, *The Journey of Adulthood,* 7th ed. (Upper Saddle River, NJ: Prentice-Hall, 2010).

6. Foster, *Celebration of Discipline,* 1.

Chapter 16: Know Thyself

1. John Calvin, *Institutes of Christian Religion* 1.1.3.

2. Saint Augustine, *Confessions* 10.3.

3. Blaise Pascal, as quoted in Peter Scazzero, *The Emotionally Healthy Church,* 81.

4. Emilie Griffin, as quoted in Richard Foster, *Prayer: Finding the Heart's True Home* (New York: HarperCollins, 1992), 8.

5. Foster, *Prayer,* 8.

6. James L. Snyder, *The Life of A. W. Tozer: In Pursuit of God* (Ventura, CA: Regal, 2009), 130.

7. Ronald A. Heifitz and Marty Linsky, *Leadership on the Line: Staying Alive Through the Dangers of Leading* (Boston: Harvard Business School, 2002), 51ff.

8. Stephen R. Covey, *The 7 Habits of Highly Effective People* (New York: Free Press, 2004), 135.

9. Daniel Goldman, *Emotional Intelligence: Why It Can Matter More than IQ* (New York: Bantam, 2006).

10. Ibid., 81.

Chapter 17: Learn

1. Peter Drucker, *Management Challenges for the 21st Century* (New York: HarperCollins, 1999), 163.

2. Stephen R. Covey, *Principle-Centered Leadership* (New York: Fireside, 1990), 33.

3. Mark H. McCormack, *What They Don't Teach You at Harvard Business School: Notes from a Street-Smart Executive* (New York: Bantam, 1984), xi–xii.

4. Marcum, Smith, and Khalsa, *Business Think*.

5. Ibid.

6. Ronald A. Heifetz and Marty Linsky, "Managing Yourself," *Harvard Business Review*, June 2002.

Chapter 18: Keep Doing the Right Things

1. Richard Nixon, *In the Arena: A Memoir of Victory, Defeat, and Renewal* (New York: Pocket, 1991).

2. Buster Olney, "Star of the Night: This Time It's Pettitte," *New York Times*, August 1998.

3. Harvey Mackay, *Swim with the Sharks without Being Eaten Alive* (New York: Ballantine, 1988), 57.

4. Sam Walton with John Huey, *Made in America: My Story* (New York: Bantam, 1993), 45.

5. Bill Parcells, *Finding a Way to Win: The Principles of Leadership, Teamwork, and Motivation* (New York: Doubleday, 1995).

6. Jon Krakauer, *Into Thin Air* (New York: Anchor, 1999), 7–8.

7. Ibid., 83.

8. Les Parrott III, *Counseling and Psychotherapy*, 2nd ed. (n.p.: Brooks Cole, 2002).

Chapter 19: Be an Actor

1. Eugene H. Peterson, *Christ Plays in Ten Thousand Places* (Grand Rapids, MI: Wm. B. Eerdmans, 2005), 52.

2. Miller, *Discipling Nations*, 275.

3. Sire, *The Universe Next Door*, 31–32.

4. Miller, *Discipling Nations*, 225, 262.

5. Robinson, *How Ronald Reagan Changed My Life*, 116.

6. Robert W. Bradford and J. Peter Duncan with Brian Tarcy, *Simplified Strategic Planning: A No-Nonsense Guide for Busy People Who Want Results Fast!* (Worcester, MA: Chandler House, 2000), 4.

7. T. Irene Sanders, *Strategic Thinking and the New Science* (New York: Free Press, 1998), 52.

Chapter 20: Be the Miracle

1. Carly Fiorina, *Tough Choices: A Memoir* (New York: Portfolio, 2006), 200–201.

2. C. S. Lewis, *Mere Christianity* (New York: HarperCollins, 1952), 131.

3. C. S. Lewis, *Perelandra* (New York: Scribner, 1996), 121.

4. Ibid.

5. Ibid., 120.

6. Ibid.

Chapter 21: The Obligation of Leadership

1. Richard L. Daft, *The Leadership Experience*, 4th ed. (Mason, OH: Thomson, 2008), 38.

2. James M. Kouzes and Barry Z. Posner, *Leadership Practices Inventory: Self Edition*, 3rd ed. (San Francisco: Pfeiffer, 2003).

3. Bill Hybels, interview with Bono, presented at Willow Creek Association Leadership Summit, August 2006.

4. DuPree, *Leadership Jazz*, 10.

5. Malcolm S. Knowles, Elwood F. Holton III, and Richard A. Swanson, *The Adult Learner: The Definitive Classic in Adult Education and Human Resource Development*, 6th ed. (San Diego, CA: Elsevier, 2005).

Chapter 22: A Place Called Willingness

1. Vaclav Havel, *Disturbing the Peace* (New York: Vintage Books, 1991), 72.

2. Soren Kierkegaard, *The Journals of Kierkegaard* (NY: Harper Torchbooks, 1959), August 1, 1835 entry.

Chapter 23: What Leaders Do

1. Warren Bennis and Burt Nanus, *Leaders: Strategies for Taking Charge* (New York: HarperCollins, 2003), 4.

2. Peter Drucker, *The 21 Irrefutable Laws of Leadership: Follow Them and People Will Follow You* (Nashville, Thomas Nelson, 2007), 18–19.

3. David McCullough, *1776* (New York: Simon & Schuster, 2005), 293.

4. Ibid., 225.

5. Ibid., 285–286.

6. Ibid., 293.

7. Seth Godin, *Linchpin* (New York: Portfolio, 2010).

8. James M. Kouzes and Barry Z. Posner, *The Leadership Challenge: How to Keep Getting Extraordinary Things Done in an Organization* (San Francisco: Jossey-Bass, 1995).

9. Ibid.

10. Sir Walter Scott, *The Talisman* (San Fancisco: Wildside Press, 2002).

11. Bennis and Nanus, *Leaders*, 95.

12. Daft, *The Leadership Experience*, 362.

13. Edmund Morris, *Theodore Rex* (New York: Random House, 2002), 308.

14. Ibid., 75.

15. Daniel A. Brown, PhD, "What Hinders Discipleship in the Church," *Commended to the World* (blog), accessed March 18, 2011, http://ctw. coastlands.org/read/articles/what-hinders-discipleship-in-church/.

16. Ibid.

17. Peck, *The Road Less Traveled*, 153.

18. Ibid., 111.

Chapter 24: What Leaders Do It For

1. Michael Z. Hackman and Craig E. Johnson, *Leadership: A Communication Perspective*, 5th ed. (Long Grove, IL: 2009), 152.

2. Ibid., 142.

3. DuPree, *Leadership Jazz*, 75.

4. Michael K. Deaver, *A Different Drummer: My Thirty Years with Ronald Reagan* (New York: HarperCollins, 2001), 32.

5. DuPree, *Leadership Jazz*, 121.

6. Marshall Goldsmith, Laurence Lyons, and Alyssa Freas, eds., *Coaching for Leadership: How the World's Greatest Coaches Help Leaders Learn* (San Francisco: Jossey-Bass, 2000), xi–xiii.

7. Fyodor Dostoyevsky, *The Brothers Karamazov*, Modern Library Edition (New York: Random House, 1996), 59.

8. Goldsmith, Lyons, and Freas, *Coaching for Leadership*, 96.

9. Ibid.

10. Ibid.

11. Anne Lamott, *Traveling Mercies: Some Thoughts on Faith* (New York: Random House, 1999), 55.

12. Jack Welch, *Winning* (New York: HarperBusiness, 2005), 79.

13. Mary Parker Follett, *The New State* (n.p.: Longmans, Green, and Co., 1918).

Chapter 25: Who Leaders Are

1. Warren Bennis and Patricia Ward Biederman, *Organizing Genius: The Secrets of Creative Collaboration* (New York: Perseus, 1997), 158.

2. Vines, *Vine's Expository Dictionary*.

3. Daft, *The Leadership Experience,* 173.

4. Craig E. Johnson, *Meeting the Ethical Challenges of Leadership: Casting Light or Shadow* (Thousand Oaks, CA: Sage, 2009), 8.

5. Lord Acton in a letter dated April, 1887, to Bishop Mandell Creighton.

6. Charles Colson, *God and Government* (Grand Rapids, MI: Zondervan, 2007).

Chapter 26: Who Leaders Are Leading For

1. Elisabeth Elliot, *These Strange Ashes* (New York: Harper & Row, 1975), 132.

Chapter 27: Stuff Happens

1. W. Warner Burke, *Organization Change: Theory and Practice,* 3rd ed. (Thousand Oaks, CA: Sage, 2011), 12.

2. McCullough, *John Adams,* 1.

3. Ibid., 9.

4. Ibid.

Chapter 28: Take Courage with You

1. Fiorina, *Tough Choices,* 98.

Chapter 30: Yes, We Will!

1. Peter Scazzero, *Emotionally Healthy Spirituality,* 29.

KEEP GETTING BETTER AT LIFE!

There is even more for you! Hopefully reading *TEN* has opened you to the futures that are inside you—futures that you are now becoming more aware of. You can continue to explore the synergy between personal growth and leading others and the essential, cyclical bond between self-help and others-help. Get better at your life, and help others get better at theirs. Continue the *TEN* experience at:

www.livingten.com

- Watch inspirational talks by Terry A. Smith
- Continue the conversation with others who are getting better at life
- Access additional resources
- Sign up to receive even more *TEN* insights

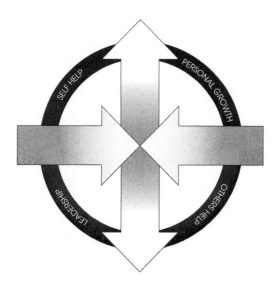